The Journal of the Reluctant Butterfly

Tales of wonder and Blood

Andrew Quilliam Brewer

This work is gratefully

dedicated to

BabaNeemKaroli

Maharaj

By whose blessing

It has emerged

Dina Bandu   Dina Nath

I wish to gratefully thank and acknowledge:

Joan Doyle   For Her magnificent cover art

Once again Joan, you have brought the beauty of your soul into the bright land   Where all that is good

Remains.

Bless you for your radiant vision, and your glowing art.

Dr Don Dudley Bushnell

Uncle, you are always there,
rousing me with inspiration
And fortitude, that I may do the
work. Thank you always for
being your wonderful Self.

**Xaviar Shivayah Alexander
Kanaio Brewer**

Zavi, you are always the magic
hands behind the work
Making it Real and may
Ganesha shine upon you soon.

The Journal of the

Reluctant Butterfly

Tales of Wonder   and Blood

First Published By
INGRAM SPARK

Ingram Spark

Ashville, NC 2022

ISBN:

9798218128951

Cover Art by Joan Doyle
Theartristyoflife.com

Other Books by Quilliam

The wings of the

resplendent

A thrilling   quiescence

        Of scarlet and   blue

Roused in a splendor of light

        In a green dawn

deep as emeralds

Filled with the dancing of rubies   and night

        And soon to be now

    The dancing of you

Deep in the wonder

of scarlet   and blue

Into this wonder we arise

Softly and gently

Unknown to ourselves

All that we have ever been

We have forgotten

Sadly, we remember only

moments like a splash of color

Thrown in haste, upon the wall

From out the madness

Of creations flurry

To be forever real

This is our prayer

Table of contents

Author's Introduction

This is the journal of a shaman.

In it, I have recounted some of the more bizarre and strange encounters I have had with the insect world, as well as the world in general. The insect world is a world unto itself.

Many years ago, a man named Eugene Marais wrote an amazing book, truly one of a kind, called " Soul of *The White Ant*." It was so much more than just scientific observation. A truly inspiring report on life. It is in the same spirit, that I offer this work to you.

The beginning

When I was five years old. I lived in Cherry Point, North Carolina, deep in the woods with my family. My father was a Marine Corps fighter pilot with a corsair squadron that was stationed there.

As it was the early fifties, there was nothing there but a field to land on. The squadron was told to build their own homes. A road was bull dozed into the deep pine forest, and everyone did just that.

My mother, who only wanted to be a writer, was very busy with two new babies at the time. So, I was left on my own to roam in the woods, with my dog.

This was a situation I was very happy with , and I would spend all day roaming in the deep woods. I would always get very lost, of course.

At first, I tried talking to the birds, but soon found them to be useless as far as practical information went, as was my dog. He was in it for his own adventure.

It was only the wind that would always lead me home at the end of the day. Thus began a lifetime of love and appreciation for the wind, and my first real shamanic adventures as well.

Of course, I knew nothing of shamanism, nor did my parents.

It was not until my late thirties that I managed to get some light shed on this subject.

I had made it a point to attend the full moon sweats given by a Karoc medicine chief named Charly Tom. He had a sweat lodge built in a small town in California, called Stewart Springs. It was located directly under the mystical and very powerful, Mt. Shasta.

I had heard a rumor of an authentic Apache medicine woman coming to one of the sweats. I managed to get a few moments with her, and I asked her what the hell was going on with my weird life.

I had a lifetime of strange experiences with animals, and thunder beings, and wind and weather of all kinds. I was hoping she could help me to understand.

She only laughed at me. She told me that first of all, real shamans are not made by any study. They are only born. She said that you can study till the crows come home, but it will not make you a real shaman.

Then she looked me deep in the eyes, and she said, it was very rare, in her experience, for a white man to be born a shaman. Then she said, "The only real question is, do you have the balls to be who you actually are?" And then she laughed.

She also told me that every shaman was born with different kinds of gifts. She said that I would have to learn how to use mine, which clearly, I had.

And then she said, "And good luck trying to explain it to anyone, because they would never believe you anyway."

   So now that I am old, and have nothing more to lose, I thought I would share some of the more interesting aspects of my shamanic life. Who knows, maybe it will help others in the same kind of situation, to understand their own life a little better.

   That being said, I offer you my journal for your amusement and consideration.

A journal that I would have to put in the nonfiction section of the library.

 Although, I have taken some poetic license to be sure. I am a poet after all.

But I have been true to the heart of the work. The heart of my story is to inspire a reverence for life.

This is its "kokoro." Fundamentally this requires openness, curiosity, and holding a space of nonjudgement about life in general.

It is about finding yourself in supreme equality with everything, Stone people, trees, plants, insects, and all forms of the manifest world.

At their root, they are all just consciousness. It all begins and ends, with consciousness. In the world of today, we believe that all form and matter is made of energy, of one form or another.

I would have to say, that based on my experience, all form arises from consciousness, is made of consciousness, and is, despite all appearances to the contrary, pure Awareness manifest to our eyes and minds, as matter.

When pure Awareness becomes self-aware, then it becomes consciousness. That is an important point to remember.

Author Koestler, in his great work "The Roots of Coincidence," mentions a friend of his that was a Noble prize-winning physicist.   He had been studying the smallest atoms in a cloud chamber, and he mentioned that if he had to say what they were composed

21

of, he would have to say
"consciousness."

I thought that was an amazing statement from a particulate nuclear physicist. Especially a Noble prize winning one.

At any rate, you may call this form of journal, a "haibun," which is a Japanese style that was transformed and made famous by Basho, the great haiku master.

In fact, you may call it whatever you like.

Proceed forward with an open mind And blessings be upon you.

Andrew Quilliam Brewer

Samurai Blue

Today was soft, but it had a wild edge.

I was sitting on the porch and watching the world ,

Before me, a butterfly, all black winged like the black knight, with blue across the bottom of his wings, came rushing at the small junco who was pulling at the dandelion in front of me.

I was almost mesmerized by the intensity of the blue upon him.

The bird was understandably surprised. It jumped back startled and gave a chirp.   The butterfly circled around and came back again, wings flailing in his face.

Now this junco here is no slouch. but the   butterfly was just too weird. And to much

He rose up and pecked back but his heart just wasn't in it. Finally, Samurai Blue, does a tight circle round and comes full on, wings up high, right in the face of junco the brave.

It was too much for the poor bird,
it pushed him over the edge of his
reality, and he just flew away.
Besides, there was nothing left there
of any interest, anyway.

Samurai Blue did a victory lap
around his small field of grass and the
few dandelions that grew there and
whatever else was there that made him
defend it with his life.

Then he returned to the small clump
of needles that was his home in the
pine tree , just above the meadow that
called so to his being like the sirens of
old.

The ways of the heart are
mysterious and bold. Who are we to

question the brave heart, now revealed, even in the body of a butterfly .

Truly, it was more than that of course. It was the man himself. When Great Spirit put the soul of a consummate samurai, who had managed to turn his last one hundred lives, into some form of samurai training, into the body of a butterfly, it made perfect sense.

How could you possibly become a samurai as a butterfly? His spirit needed a rest and badly, and the body of a large black butterfly with striking blue wings seemed the perfect solution.   What could you possibly do wrong as a butterfly after all?

Well, it was just revealed that the body matters not when the spirit is strong.   So, **Samurai Blue** was born. And with those stripes of blue, he will strike you down if you annoy him, so be warned.   He is so much more, than he seems.

The Porch

Spiders , and beetles, and tigers   Oh my

Suddenly I found myself in a state of mind that was rare indeed, even for a shaman.

When I gazed upon the insects that would crawl out upon my porch

I could hear them.

They sang within my mind and their strange stories were revealed to all who would listen. I was amazed, yet I was very curious to hear what they said.

The first was the story from a very large spider that just walked right up in front of me and told me the following:

GERONIMO'S   STORY

"When I awoke into my mind, a shout called forth my spirit. Geronimo, it rang and thundered. Geronimo, I remembered. And then I awoke into this body , a spider's body, and already I knew the thirst for blood was deep within me. I was surprised. The man I was had faded far away, but not forgotten.

I knew at once that it mattered not the size or shape a spirit may become. What mattered was the heart within.

My heart was strong as ever I was as a man. I have thundered through my life as a spider. I have drunk the blood of many who were also men.

I noticed that many of them were, of the army that slaughtered most of my people.

I would always tell them before they died, it is Geronimo that drinks your blood now. It is the red man's victory that now at last prevails.

All is balance in the eyes of the Great Spirit, and a great imbalance was brought upon my people. Now I battle it, one by one. I strike you down one by one. I drink your blood, and now you have become my blood.

My blood is true. My blood is stronger. My blood has joined with the Earth and seen the light within. You men who murdered my children, now you have looked into the eyes of death, and you have seen the heart break you brought upon my people.

Now your blood is my blood. Now you have become a Red Man, and so you will be born again into a red man's body. You will suffer, as the red man still suffers at the hands of the white demons, until you finally change, and know that all men are the same.

The Creator smiles upon each soul with equal light.   But know this. In this world of the crawling creatures, and the sweat born, and the egg born, the red man will prevail. The earth haters will be eaten until their demon form, and the demon within him, will disappear from the face of the earth at last.

This is my work, and I revel in your blood.

I watch the fear in your eyes as death comes upon you. I tell you now, as I drink your blood. The red man is upon the earth and within the earth and has many forms. Your bones will still be fresh when the last of your kind is eaten and turned into the true blood. The red blood is the true blood of the earth.

The earth haters with all their demons, will finally be taken away and transformed, and balance will be restored, and so at last men may enter this world as equals.

Hear my words. We of the earth will prevail upon the earth, long after your machines and your poisons have disappeared. Spirit will rise to

restore the balance and the tyranny
of the demon race will be no more.

You will not prevail against the
spirit of the Mother who gave you life
and the Father who gave you form.
The Earth will rise up and take back
her own at last.

Soon, I will be free again, to be
born as a man. Full knowing that I
have devoured and transformed a
great horde of the army of the men
that overran my people while I lived
as a man.

Living on the earth and in the earth,
I have seen the wonders that all men
seek to know and find. The gold and

the hidden jewels. Yet these glories
are all of the living spirit and are the
embodiment of wisdom, as gold is
truth itself.   So are these glories kept
away from the men who seek only to
horde them for power and abuse
them. They are the earth's delight
and treasure, made to bring the
deeper beauty into form.

I have walked among the earth's
treasures, and I have seen the greed
in the eyes of the demon kind as they
crawl among them. Even still they
hunger for treasure and glory. Even
as I drink their blood, they reach out
for gold.

Yet it is I, Geronimo, that stands among the treasures with a reverent heart.

I bow to the Mother for her kind generosity and her willingness to share with all, the deeper beauty of existence.

This is the wisdom of the Red Man, long before the whites brought their demon water to confuse our minds and spirits.

This Mother, I love. And when I walk again as a man, I will not forget my journey as a spider being. My soul will be refreshed by the blood of ten thousand demons, who are now transformed.

I will retrieve my Stones from the sacred three fingers where I hid them, and I will come again to lead my people from tyranny and the oppression of the demon race. Spirit will prevail, and the Red Man will rise again to honor the Mother, and reclaim the earth from the treachery of the abomination that fights to over come her.

This have I seen

This I know to be the Real and the true.

Do not despair, my brothers and sisters, the Earth will be Red again, and all will at last come into balance, and so at last be free from this devil that may infect any man, and any race. I have fought against this demon for many lifetimes, and I will never stop until it is finally removed from the hearts of the people.

Freedom is above us and below us and all around us. Freedom is now the road we will walk upon. Freedom has come back to the earth, and we who love this earth, will overcome

at last.

I was of course, rather stunned by his passion. I was very tempted to edit his words, they seemed so strong.   But in the end, I decided that I am just the reporter, so I should have the courage to just report it as honestly as I can.

So, I just let it ride in, on my soul, come what may.

The real Geronimo of course was an amazing shaman. He had powers and abilities far beyond the normal shaman. He could never be killed by a bullet, and he was a master of coyote medicine. At one time he hid hundreds of his warriors in and around a large cliff while literally thousands of cavalries were hunting for him.

His medicine stones he took with him and buried , he never passed them on. When he was younger his whole family was murdered and most of his people.

His rage against the white man, and the Mexicans never ended.   It is easy to understand why he felt such vehemence and why he and his warriors enacted such terrible vengeance upon the invading whites.

In the end, he finally surrendered in order to save what was left of his people. He never could adjust to reservation life.

If this was indeed the spirit of Geronimo in this large spider, I could understand his passion.

As a shaman I have felt it rise like a fire within me from the destruction I see all around, and the terrible loss of so many endangered species .

The next story came from a very large
South American Hercules beetle,
which I was very amazed to see.

THE HERCULES BEETLE' S STORY

" I am the largest of my kind. I am
the strongest and I am the greatest of
all the conquering wonders of this
world.

My present form matters nothing.
I know who I am. I know what I have
done. I remember everything, and I
regret nothing. There are very few
who can say that.

Surprisingly now there are many who walk as sweat born or egg born in this world. I now claim the allegiance of many great and formidable warriors who still roam this earth.   And still they fight, and still they die. I am the greatest of my kind. I am the Khan.

I was once Gangues the Khan and I fear no man nor beast nor any creature that ever lived or breathed air.

Though now I am reduced in size, I still destroy all within my reach. I am the Reapers Reaper.   I am the jaws of death. Though I may be small in this world, I am not diminished.

My spirit will stand up to any man who ever lived. Save those few holy men that live in that other world. In this world, I have no equal.

But now there is no vengeance in my heart. My heart is quiet

I never killed a being that surrendered to me first. Only those who resisted my conquest. I let all religions and all customs continue as long as they gave me tribute and obeyed my laws.

I cared nothing for their ways. I let them all continue. I asked only for tribute and obeisance, nothing more.

I forced no man or race to change their nature or religion. I let them all do as they would, as long as they obeyed my laws. Few conquerors of the world can make that claim. "

Needless to say, I was understandably surprised as it lumbered away.

Next up, a much smaller and very pretty green, Eastern Hercules beetle arrived on the scene and proceeded to tell me her story.

THE SMALL BEETLES STORY.

My name is Illama. I am now a beetle. I was a quiet woman and a writer. I was nothing special in my life. I have heard the boastful and fanciful prattling's of many insects who have claimed to be this or that.

Mostly, they are all liars, and deeply deluded. It is the trademark of many insects to be deluded and filled with a blood lust. . When they were human, they were also deluded and filled with a hunger for power and blood.

I believe the spider Geronimo; he seems actually genuine. But the Khan, seems like just a big brute to me.

So many insects are very brutish and full of hunger for something. I myself am just happy to be alive again. I eat the plants and the bark, and I am content just to see the world once more.

To my surprise, I have found that the insect world is mostly no different from the world of men. They were all brutes and liars, and they have not changed at all as far as I can tell.

There is many a woman that I have known, that would say **amen** to that, I was tempted to say.

Many months later and living in a completely different house, although still in the same country, I again had another moment with the insects.

I had been sitting on my porch again and setting up my alter on one side on the railing, overlooking the bird feeding station.

I noticed an extremely large daddy long legs. The biggest I had ever seen. Over the next few weeks, he kept showing up on my radar, even crawling over my head, which I did not appreciate. Fortunately, he was not injured when I brushed him off.

The next day he got himself trapped on my alter railing and could not get past, it seemed. He finally settled on my large incense box, and I saw the opportunity to let him go off the porch.

Several days later he reappeared, right next to my alter , and just sat there.

I realized that he was trying to communicate with me, so I said "Ok." I looked right at him, and I said," if you have a story, I will write it. " Then I closed my eyes and went into a kind of meditation.

When I awoke, the spider was gone, but I knew there had been some kind of a transmission. Shortly thereafter, the following story just poured out of me.

THE AWAKENED SKULL SPIDERS STORY

"Least of all, did I expect to roam this world as a large spider. Yet here I am. Here I am and I am forever confused

to be this now. Still, I can begin to understand why. I can remember my last strange life. It seemed I was pretty ruthless as a man, devoid of compassion and even of generosity, for the most part. Now , I can see the matter more clearly, and I began to hope again for a better way to be.

The spider's way is very simple and brutal, and yet there are many out there that I kill and eat that were once, like myself.

Sometimes we even talk as men, trapped by our fate. But I notice the result is always the same. Although I do enjoy the chance to converse with another being, who is bound like myself in an insect's body.

Amazing to me how many of those I met are either politicians or bankers, or lawyers.

They are usually very surprised to be just another meal for me.

Death is more unreal as a spider. It is just the natural way of things, no big deal. Rarely do I hear them protest their fate.

Although the famous ones often mistakenly believe that they are still famous in some remote way, or that I will be somehow impressed.

I am never impressed. I feel like the hooded figure of death in an old Bergman movie.

Yet I wonder what it is I am supposed to be learning from this life. It seems so short and direct really. Although I do have long periods of just being in the day and just waiting. It is actually very peaceful.

Perhaps that is the lesson here to be learned, the deep peace that abides everywhere in life. I feel more peace now as a spider, then I ever did as a man. Pretty strange really

Now Suddenly, I am remembering the sea the Sea. It breaks and crests upon my breast and makes me bold and free. Still the poet

I notice ,   Even as a spider.

I still can see the dawn light as it beaks upon my sails, all set and full of wind. I was happy then and felt as if I never would be chained again. I am very happy to remember now, how I loved the Sea.

It is very hard, when you are a spider to not believe that you have always been a spider and will always be a spider. To have lived once in another body, that is almost a dream beyond imagining.

That is the trap you see. This is what you think you must believe to the very core of your being, but that is

the very reason why you are now a
spider.

The inflexible and irrefutable belief
that you stand now as the truth of
who you are, that is the very reason,
it seems, for this reality to exist.

It is true, that I am now a spider.
But I do know, to the very core of my
being, that I have lived many
different lives and been many
different things and beings and
forms.

I even once, had a wake-up
moment when suddenly I knew I was
not a body or a thing, because

existence was not my real domain at
all.   Surprise   Surprise.

     So, now and I a m , thankfully,
actually aware, most of the time.

     When I realized that I had an
opportunity to be heard by you, I
decided to take it.

     It seems strange, but this act has
changed my life, or at least my mind.
When I saw that I had a chance to
speak, a strong spirit moved suddenly
within me and just came pouring out.

     I have been having a pretty good
life as a spider. It is easy pickings for

a tall spider with a powerful bite. I
need very little to sustain myself. It is
a very monk like existence.

Reminds me very much of my life
as a monk. It is of course much more
direct and brutal, but it is without all
the anxiety and doubt and remorse.

It is also without all the very
frustrated sexual energy that I felt as
a monk that almost drove me insane.
So, all things being equal, I would
choose the spider body, any day.

Once you have, at least to some
degree, broken free from beliefs of
any kind. Once you have tapped the
touch stone of yourself, even a little,

***freedom takes on
a whole new meaning.**

The first freedom is to be able to
move between the forms. Sort of like
interchangeable belief patterns, that
you can just slip on.

So, for instance, you can bring all
your many frustrations that come
from the belief that you are a man, or
a woman, and plunk them all down in
the body of a skull spider.

The result is often very liberating.
Almost like getting high, it is very
similar in fact, almost intoxicating.

But unfortunately, all the same
karmic disasters follow you,

whatever form you have taken. That is really the fundamental problem.

It seems to me that there are very few young souls now. They are all mostly old and full of baggage.

We seem to carry all the same baggage, like stones upon our back,

Endlessly, and forever, until we finally truly decide to let it all go, or to transform it.

In order to do that however, unless you are very lucky, you need to have taken" Waking up   101."   This class is a required prerequisite.

Most people are still in elementary school when it comes to any understanding about the art and practice of waking up, sad to say.

You only have to look around you, not at the invisible ones, but the ones that are kept in the limelight.

That tells you everything you need to know about the current condition of the human race.

That is probably why the big **zero** event is well on the way.

I am guessing, water this time, but I am not a prophet. The result will be the same anyway.

I do feel in my bones , that those of us who will be sticking around

To keep the dance going, will be
profoundly   Us.

Personally, I am looking forward to it.
It sounds like fun to me.

Sometimes, I have moments when
I can remember back. Must be at
least 15 million years ago now. But
there is no sense of time in these
memories. Just seems like yesterday
almost.

That was some truly crazy times. I
mean, mind bending, and bizarre.
Please, don't even get me started.
Let's just say some mighty big ass
giants were only a small part of the
mix, in those days.

Many of us here today were around then. But very few can remember. I find that it is definitely more fun to be able to remember, but only if you want to. Most prefer not to remember.

I can relate to that of course. But now, having attained to a certain degree of formlessness, at least in my belief systems, I can really enjoy the memories of my past lives, much more.

I have let go of most of them by now. I do know that love endures beyond form. Then memory becomes more like a set of watercolors, or oil paints. Especially if it is used as a means of expression for the Art of Being.

The Art of Being is a very Zen kind of thing.

More like a song that finds its own chorus in the symphony of existence.

Words can't quite get there. And it makes no sense at all to a spider who never bothers with words, anyway.

Now a spider who used to be a poet, well that is a different kind of a problem.

But I am enjoying myself, for the most part. I would never have thought it possible when I was a human. But I am actually enjoying myself, at least, for now. And we all

know just how brief that "for now "
part really is.

For the record, I wouldn't mind
being a giant again, well maybe not.

But you can see how the mind can
just run away with itself when you
can remember everything.

I rest my case. "

*Many years earlier in my life, I had
had a few encounters with the insect
world. None quite so compelling or
deep. That is a very rare event.*

*And somewhat unsettling to be
honest.*

We are talking about taking consciousness to the quantum level to be sure. Hardly believable to most , unless you yourself have roamed through these strange waters, deep waters, very deep and down in the trench at the bottom of the world , kind of waters.

But I digress.

I had just returned from England, and I was dead broke. My father had a small piece of land that was very wild, in the hills above Half Moon Bay , in California.   That was in the early 80 s, and there was little or no construction going on.   From the top of my hill, I could see a straight shot twenty miles down to the sea.

It was truly a remote and wild area. I pitched a small tent for a home and managed to find work occasionally with my old friend Patrick, doing construction. Two days a week was all the money I needed in those days.

I had decided to pitch my tent on a small clear section of the property. Like a complete idiot, I did not notice that it was right in the middle of a trail used by a local cougar.

I became aware of this one night when I suddenly awoke

and heard a very distinct but low growling.

I was immediately concerned and sat up to look out the small window in the top of my tent.

The minute I started to move towards the window, the growling increased in volume dramatically. I stopped and waited and listened carefully. and did not move.

The growling continued as the cat slowly made her way across the lot, directly in front of my tent.

Finally, I could stand it no more and I began to very slowly raise my head up to the window. I even held my breath. The minute I began to move, the cat gave out a final warning that was very loud and very direct. "If you look at me, you die".   I had no doubts about the situation, or the communication.

I immediately just stopped and breathed.   I did not even move a hair.

Finally, I could hear the cat had moved far enough away, but I still did not look at her. I got the full intent of her meaning.

It was then that I began to understand how extremely psychic and connected a mountain lion is.

She could see and sense even the smallest movement. Had I moved again, even the slightest towards the window, or had I felt any inclination towards defending myself, I would have been instantly dead.

The cat could sense that I had no hostility towards her. That was definitely a mark in my favor. As long as I did not violate her boundary of not being seen. I was allowed to live.

Our thoughts became connected on a very primal level. I could feel and sense her, and she could feel and know all my thoughts completely. I had no doubt about that at all.

When I emerged the next morning, I realized I had camped directly on her trail, like a fool.

Down the mountain about half a mile, I could see where she lived. There was a cluster of granite boulders that rose up, surrounded by poison oak and nettles.

Somewhere in there she had found a cave. There was nothing man made for many miles in every direction. A perfect spot for a cougar.

I wisely decided to move my camp over to the other side of the lot.

When I walked closer to her cave to look around some more, I suddenly noticed the bees.

At first it seemed normal, but very busy.

Then after a few more steps, I looked ahead and saw a world of bees that I had never even, in my lifetime , remotely dreamed of.   It seemed to occupy, maybe an acre of ground.

There were no trees, only sage and some wild bushes with flowers, and bright and shiny crystalline stones.

It was very hard to even see the ground. The entire area was deeply covered with many hives of bees. How many I could not say, but at least 15, in the immediate proximity.

It was an **intensity** of bees .

Yet they were all staying close together within their own zones.

The energy of the place itself seemed to vibrate and hum along with the bees. The extreme volume of bee sound was almost impossible to listen to. It was completely unnerving.

I suddenly lost all sense of separateness, I was in some kind of deep unity, but the energy was rather intense, and

 it was very strange.   I felt a profound awareness of my being, like I was being watched. .

Of all the hives of bees around me, I think I noticed the bumble bees the most.   They were definitely the loudest.

Suddenly, a huge chunk of the hive flew directly at my head.

My reaction was just shock and awe, and fortunately I did not move.

Thankfully, they veered up at the last minute and just grazed my brow, and then were gone.

I turned around immediately and made my way out of the hive zone. I wasn't experiencing a lot of fear, just complete awe, and gratitude for being allowed to live.

I did understand that part very well. If the roles had been reversed, the bees probably would all be dead. So yes, I was very grateful that they had allowed me to live and to leave.

The sheer immensity of the consciousness that was there in the form of an **intensity** of bees, defies description.   I have never seen anything like it.

As I walked back up to my tent, I surveyed the scene I had just walked through. The first layer was the zone of bees, completely impenetrable, followed closely by a zone of thorns and huge poison oak bushes. In the middle of all this, was the cougars cave, somewhere inside the large granite boulders.

Very impressive .   Certainly, kept me away.

My next encounter with bee consciousness was many years later. I was living on Maui, in my new house high up on the mountain in the "bad lands" of Kanaio. It was a very remote and wild place.

My wife and I had arrived home after a leave of several days, only to find the house filled with bees. There were at least 4 hives humming behind the double walls of the old house.

I was horrified. Suddenly the house was completely uninhabitable. The prospect of battling a horde of bees with cans of spray and poison,

seemed terrible to contemplate, and
even frankly impossible.

I remembered how I had gone up
against a small hive of very angry
wasps, I had made a promise to myself
that I would never do that again.

So, I just went outside and sat next to
the house. I waited until I could feel
some kind of awareness of the bees.

Then I just spoke up. I said " please
listen up whoever is watching over
these bees. I appreciate that this is a
good place for a hive, but please
understand, they may not live here in
this house, it is already occupied.

I am going down to town now, and
I am going to buy all the most toxic

poisons I can find, and I am coming back.   I will be gone about four hours. A war is not what I want.

What I want is for everyone to be gone by the time I come back. Please consider my request.   There is no reason why we all have to die here.

There is a lot of room in Kanaio for bees.   You can go where you like, just not in my house. I am asking you with respect and gratitude so that you will do the right thing. "

I really did not know what to expect.   I think I was actually expecting the worst and I was not looking forward to it.

When we pulled back into the driveway four hours later, I stopped and listened.

Nothing. I could hear nothing. Almost in disbelief, I walked over to the house.

It was completely empty of bees.

I was overwhelmed with a sense of relief and gratitude. I carefully went through the whole house and found nothing.

I felt like I had been given my house back from an alien invasion.

Mostly what I felt was gratitude. Deep gratitude.

I suddenly developed a whole new respect for bees. It has remained with me to this day.

Giant Centipede

I believe that the most direct and very real conversation I ever had with an insect, was with a giant centipede.

 The memory of it has never left me, and it is just as vivid now, as the day it happened.

We had been living in the new house in Kanaio on Maui, for several years, and the gardens were well started and beautiful. We now had a baby, a young boy.

We were sitting in the living room and my wife suddenly said to me that she had just seen the biggest centipede of her life, crawling up the wall.

I immediately looked over, but I could see nothing.

So, of course I was somewhat skeptical in a hopeful kind of way, not wanting the baby to be in any real danger. I immediately began going through my homeopathy books looking under delusions.

That is an amazing study, by the way . Very eye opening.

Everything you need to know, is there.

However, I could find no remedy that seemed to fit, "sees giant centipedes on wall ".

Several days later, again in the living room, looking out at the new porch I had just built, we noticed that the cats were going crazy on the end of the deck.   So, I went out to have a look.

There, in plain sight, surrounded by cats, was a gigantic centipede.

He was easily 14 inches or more.   At first, I was alarmed and worried about the baby. So, I raised up my shovel intending to cut the beast in half.

But then I looked at him and marveled. I realized that he must be the king of all centipedes.

So, changing my mind momentarily, I put the shovel down next to him. I said out loud "climb on the shovel, and I will take you out of here".   To my great surprise, he did so, very quickly.

I lifted him up and walked about a hundred yards down the road, away from the house and gardens. I came to a nice rocky place, and I put him down gently.

Instead of crawling off and running away , he just went a few feet and looked at me.

So, I said to him, "let us have an accord between us. I don't care where you or your people live. I just do not want to see them, or be injured by them, and that goes for my family as well.

Go where you like, just be invisible about it. Do we have an accord? We will have peace between us, what do you say?

Quite astoundingly, that massive centipede rose up on the very end tip of his tail, standing a full foot in the air and looked at me. I looked him straight in the eye, and he in turn, looked in mine.

There was a rare moment of connection between us,

"Then, we have an accord" I said, and folded my hands in a prayerful gesture. He dropped back down and slowly crawled off into the rocks.

I was moved and very surprised by my feelings.

For the entire rest of the time, we lived in that house, we never saw any centipedes, despite major earth works in the gardens.   He kept his word with me.

He was after all, an honorable king. A very rare thing these days. I have never forgotten him.

My appreciation of centipedes was greatly magnified. I took it very personally, this oath between us.

I was very pleased that he did as well.

I had a brief moment again with the **amazing, awakened spider**. I really don't know what else to call him.

He just walked up next to my chair on the railing of the porch and hung out there. I realized that he still had more to say. We just sat together for a while, and I blew some medicine smoke in his direction, and we did some OOOMMing together. I held the thought about humor, in the spider world.

The next day, I was watching the hummingbirds in furious activity chasing off all the small birds they could. It was an early morning show with mini swordsman, that I always enjoyed.

 I had the thought that it was only because of the feeding I provided, that the birds could have the energy to spend so much of it in defense of the homeland.   It was an enormous outlay of energy and calories.

   Reminded me a lot of the human race.

   Then I realized I needed to go inside and write some more of his strange story. And so, I did.

The story continued:

" I spent a large part of my last life, as a man on Wall street.   Wall street in its original form. It is very strange to me that so many of those I knew and knew of, found themselves in the realm of spiders.

It is often , with great satisfaction, that I discover a banker friend that I knew. Especially one that was grandiose and of an aggravating composition. Especially when he can recognize me, and I can recognize him. We are able to somehow see, through the illusion that is now between us.

So, I say, "now Fitzgerald old sod, I am really going to enjoy our lunch together, far more than I ever did when you were gleefully making my life a misery. I will go slow, and let you consider just how much grief and pain that now I can bring to you. In the light of all you did to me, it seems completely fair.

What's that you say ?, You are hoping to renegotiate our present arrangement?

I think not, old sanctimonious slime bob, I think not. Not even in a million years when I am mellow tempered and well fed, I will still enjoy the agony of you, in fact, I will go further even, I will write about it.

As did my old friend Jonathan , when the English were so righteously proclaiming their self-evident superiority.

He and Gulliver (why am I not surprised) ,had the very last word in that encounter, and I will as well, with you.

You see. The poets will always be victorious in the end. It is the natural order of evolution. As it should be.

I believe I will have *you raw* and *wiggling* on the fork.

Raw as the lies you fed me then.

Your untimely end is now completely at the mercy of my mouth. As my end was once in yours. And I intend to savor it now, yea, that is the humor of spiders.

Since someone has asked so nicely.

I will savor you now with glee and a chuckle, perhaps even a laugh, a belly laugh in fact would be appropriate.

And that is one of the more humorous sides , of being a spider."

" You were wondering about humor.   Did it even exist?

An interesting question.

The spider body offers strange opportunities. But I must proclaim that humor is always in the man, if he is alive at all.

If his spirit lives, he must have laughter in his soul.

The humor that I have experienced is very much of the kind that Dante must have felt when he wrote Paradise lost.

There is a lot of revenge kind of humor, and the satisfaction of seeing things become more balanced up, so to speak. It is very much all about justice, and the re balancing of events.   So that they finally do come into balance in the end. "

I felt like we had finally come to an understanding or sorts.   At least a kind of completion. He had given me a lot to think over.

I had been noticing for some days now a very large spider that lived in a very tight web on the roof above me.

Not a widow, I knew, but larger than the daddy long legs, and more wolf like, though not as big as a wolf spider, and much skinnier.

I noticed that she always kept hidden away behind her web when I was there. After I had finished with the daddy long legs, I looked up again, and there she was, in all her glory, looking down at me.

I felt like she was curious about me and what I was doing.

So, I said ,” well I am available if you
are.”

The next day the transmission just
came out.

The scary spiders story

**I will talk to you. I was never a
human, at least not from this planet.**

I was a woman born as a high priestess from a land you have never heard of.

Not human, but certainly more conscious than most humans I have ever seen.

I am interested in this strange kind of connection that is possible, between the species. I have never seen it before, although I have heard about it.

It is in our stories of shape shifters; you would call them.

I have heard many of your people's stories, mostly very confused and very far from the truth.

It was my job, in my priestess form, to be precise and exact in my dealings with reality.

Not like your sort.   All imagination and very muddle headed. No <u>clarity.</u>

No wonder you have brought this ruin upon yourselves. We can all see it coming. Those of us who can perceive reality with more lucidity .

Your kind is beyond all bounds of belief in a rational mind. You are all, way out of control.

But, I am watching it, at least , with interest.

We even have poets, in our world. Although they are very rare.

My brother was actually one of the best.

He had an extraordinary life, probably nothing that you could ever comprehend. It was very multi-dimensional with parallel universes and the like.   Way beyond your mental abilities, I suspect.

I saw you talking with that very arrogant daddy long legs. He would be well advised to stay far away from me.

So, I have allowed a connection between us. In the memory of my

brother. He would have enjoyed you.

Family is important to us.

I leave you now.

Well, that was pretty weird, I have to say. I am experiencing a new understanding of consciousness. That it can run very deep. As deep as the water allows. It seems that the form hardly matters as with the micro world of quarks and changing particles and waves. The time or the place hardly matters.

It is more just a moment shared between life forms.

My final thoughts on the insect world, from the point of view of a shaman.

I believe that a great many of the insect forms that I have had contact With were at one time human.

I don't think this is about karma. I think it is about what the soul needs most, in order to evolve.

From the point of view of the Buddhists , a human life is most precious and if it is wasted, then there is no reason to have it again any time soon. From my experience, a life of hatred and blame and persecution is very likely to end as an insect.

The fundamentalists, and fanatics
and all those who persecute others in
the name of God, are in for a big
surprise. The tyrants and dictators
and war mongers are also very likely
to end up with six legs.

The opportunity to have a human
life is rare and amazing.   It is mostly
wasted by the vast amount of people
who are locked into ignorance and
prejudice and the pursuit of pleasure .

To rise above all that is never easy.
But if you do, then you may get
another chance to be human, and even
possibly to be a poet.   And that is a
grand thing indeed.   It is a true
blessing.

I do believe however that poets do indeed have the final word. No matter the form, or the world they were born into.

I say Hurrah to that.

Speaking of poets,

I have discovered many piles of new poetry and some old, that are demanding to see the light of print. I am hardly in a position

To refuse them.

Enough, and be done, with the bug world I say and be gone with you all, if you please.

NEW POEMS

The Tiger

Surrounded by fools

In the sublime silence of God

I wait

 There is nothing to be said

Nothing to be done

I would sing to you

Of the majesty

In the heart

Of a tiger

Whose face I touched

In perfect trust

And he, my innocence upheld

Without hesitation or blame

For the murders and the suffering

My race has brought upon his kind

My hand upon his face

I waited

Instead, he showed me within his eyes

The unbroken line of his lineage

A lineage without shame

My hand was felt,   and then
returned

My eyes, grew wet and bright

I gazed in awe

At his perfect greatness

I gazed in awe

At the splendor of his way

I met this 900 lb. Siberian tiger in the Olympic rain forest in Washington in the eighties. Our encounter changed my life. I have never forgotten him

He still roams freely within my heart.

I have never seen or even heard of one bigger.

Poems of Hanuman   1

Let No, be alone

Let Yes, linger longer

Let your heart grow stronger

Do this, and love me   and be free

Let go around you   2

Just let it be

Whatever it already is

The mosquitoes will drink your blood

All the same, to them

Remember

All the same to them

As the black cloth plods its way   3

Into the bleeding heart, once more

To play so sweet a tune

Breaks your heart   it does

Just breaks it, right apart

Lord Piddledrum spoke at last   4

Just stop, He said

Just stop

And so of course they all did,

At once

Then the world was suddenly

Bright again. How simple was that

The razzle blum berry bum   5

Bloated all berry

He just rose up once again

And he said

Yes

Oh just yes

Oh

Just yes

  once again

In cinnamon froth did he dabble   6

too long

Alas for his family and friends

And his glistening wives, and all of

his wolves   Full   of rabbits

Well, rabbits and mice to be sure

But they all were happy to see him

just dance

To the rainbow inside of his belly

And bring forth a song

Like a whale

From the long of his row

In the loudest of ways

It burst out of his belly

Like a whale

The flower rises   7

More than I

Will ever sing my songs, again

Last of my   kind

Walking slow   into light

At the very end of time

A HAA   A HUM

A WHO

A HO   A HAA

ALWAYS a song at the end

And a laugh   for Sita

Sita   my truest love

8

When innocence is re united once
again

With love

Always there is a rejoicing

In the heart

When innocence is re united

What can we say

   but hooray

9

When the spring warmth is beginning

To un quiver   like a lover's careful
touch

It settles into the depth

Where love is true

Like a wounded weaver

Now he must question

Even the sheep

Before he will sign   Anything

The chi obelisk remembers

As there is always a memory

To return to

The tri illion resonatum   believes

And so,   becomes *that once again,*
over time

But

In the whisper of mango leaves it
comes

A maelstrom of wonder

And resolve

Like breath in the morning

It rises   when we rise

And when we rise

The world rises

Once again

On the edge always   10

Of the passion, and the joy

Each step reveals the next

No further

Each step must feel

The courage and the fire

To pass   without falling

Each step is a ladder

For the next to follow

If you fall

Many will fall

If you rise

Many may rise

You are never alone with your
courage

You are always alone   with your fear

On the edge always

Of the passion and the joy

Each step reveals the next

No further

The only question

Will you fall   or will you float,   or
will you   finally fly?

Peaches   glow green   11

In the vast   moon light

They are never worried

They live for others

And so, the birds

 love them

As do the Lords of Light

Never enough of those damn peaches
though

Just never enough

The jewels of Ram   12

The jewels of Ram

The finest in the world

I crushed in my teeth

They were ancient and holy

I threw them out

None but Ram

Or that which bears his name

My dwell with me

Ram is etched on my bones

It is imprinted

Upon the bones of my breast

I am the breath of Ram

I am the name Made into a lightning
bolt

Jai jai Ram   Jai jai Hanuman

Random thoughts

Found in the library of Self

The garden of love

Is an eternal place

It is outside of time's dimension

If you are so lucky as to find a true

love, then you must

Understand .

It is a long time in the garden that

you must spend.

It is not just one life. It is many lives.

And they are all difficult and

different.

But if you deeply understand that the garden only gets better and better, every year that you tend it, then

You can begin to understand ,   and to reap the rewards.

Some trees only bloom once, every thirteen years.

Some only bloom once , every hundred years.

Once you understand what it is to be a gardener in this garden, then you will never be disappointed .

Every year the trees grow a little taller, and the flowers a little stronger.

If you are able to stay with it, then
you will know the true joy
Of love.

Never ending, and eternal love.

And yes, you must work at it
diligently to keep the garden alive.
But the rewards are incomparable
and amazing to behold.

And you will never be sorry to be a
gardener in this garden.

THE Quantum and the ZERO POINT

You cannot arrive at zero point in the quantum field as a particle. As long as you are considering "how do I", do this?" You remain in the particulate world.

Unfortunately, the "I,s " cannot do this . Because the "I,s" are a particle in a field, as an observer of the field.

But the observer can also be more in the realm of pure awareness. At the same time. This is the quantum realm.

This is the true meaning of quantum entanglement. To deeply appreciate this is to move closer to letting go of "dualism."

Awareness can have many subtleties and shades. Mostly it is about purity. Space and purity. These are the fertile winds that nourish the newborn awareness.

The quantum awareness

To be born again, as a wave.

When I make an authentic contact with the quantum void

The result is a wave form. So now I am transformed from a particle and an observer to an expanded sense of awareness

As a wave form rises, so do I rise.

I remember riding on the waves and being in the waves and falling deep in the foam and body of the wave. Years did I spend living and loving in the waves.

So, to this form of consciousness, I can relate.

Let me give you two examples of authentic but extraordinary contact.

When Neem Karoli Baba was a boy, he used to hang around the Hanuman temples.

One day the priest had to leave briefly, so he asked the boy to take over.

His job was to just receive the food the pilgrims would give, offer it to Hanuman, and then return it as prasad (food blessed by Hanuman) to the pilgrims.

Simple enough. When the priest returned some hours later, he found a lot of very angry pilgrims. They had just chased off the boy who was stealing their food, they said.

So, the priest went on a search and found the boy and asked him what happened.

The boy (Neem Karoli) replied that he had received the food from the pilgrims and offered it to Hanuman.

But nothing happened.

So, he picked up a stick and he beat Hanuman until he took all the food.

He told the pilgrims that Hanuman had received their food, but   they didn't believe him and so they chased him off.

At that point, the priest realized that he was dealing with a very high Baba, who had just done so easily, what he had been trying to do his whole life.

The second story is from Ramakrishna.

He was talking to his disciples about the Mother.

He said that the Mother is always very busy, and she gives her children many toys to keep them happy.

And then He said, but only if you can throw down all your toys and loudly cry for the Mother, then you will finally get her attention and she will come running to you.

But you must never give up, and you must loudly and sincerely cry for Her .

Both of these stories illustrate the same thing.

That you must not settle for anything less, than an authentic connection to actual reality. When that line is crossed, the wave responds.

It is all about the level of contact.

The first step is to go beyond the enchantment of the mind. You must want to make" real" contact.

Which implies that you have decided that the other, in question, might actually be real.

It all begins with you. You must be real. You must be your most authentic self.

Then, when you reach out to another, from this place, the magic happens.

122

One of the greatest of the recent Babas, Sherdi Sai Baba, made it simple. He said, "if you look at me, then I will look at you." Everything you need to know, is right there.

Once you have managed to make an authentic contact with another, there is always a response. The form it will take depends a lot on your belief systems and your openness.

Sadly , for the most part, we are all bounded by what we believe to be true of reality. Hard to see a dragon, if you just don't believe in dragons. Its that simple.

Same goes for fairies and elves and much of magic land .

You must be willing to suspend your beliefs, you must be willing to suspend judgement.

According to the current Dali lama , this is the true meaning of love.

"Suspending judgement."

So, you must be willing to reach out from the deepest place of yourself that you know to be real, to another that you may not even know who or what they are, or if they are even real.

You must be willing to "not know" anything about this other, and still, you reach out anyway.

This is the secret. Extending a hand from your own heart, to another mysterious being that you may not even believe in. Like a tree, or a stone, or the river.

 You may have a sense of their reality, but not of their conscious reality.

Are they a living conscious being, or just a stupid rock.

Is that bug that is gazing into your eyes, a conscious being, or just a dumb insect.

You must be willing to "not know" any of the answers to these questions. You must be willing to just "do it anyway", as my old guru was very fond of saying.

You must be willing to step out of your box, and to be surprised.

A true understanding of reality starts with a true understanding of who you actually are.

None of this is easy. It does require that you make a genuine effort to go to "source" and be willing to not know anything about the reality of what you are reaching out to.

 If you are willing to do this, then you may be in for a big surprise.

Your first real contact outside of your box, is always deeply felt, and even humbling. And so now , your life will really begin with a whole new perspective.

126

The response

When we enter a new realm, as the observer of the field,

The realm   responds.

The response, opens a door

This is the place, where we tend to overlook the nature of the quantum.

In the response, is a living force

A conscious force

That living force moves through everything and becomes entangled.

The response, changes everything

Now the eternal creative moment is charged

Just like in photosynthesis

A wave is created, and it goes out looking

For the shortest path, to completion.

That is the nature of a wave

It connects to everything without lines

Just like love

Children's poem stories from the hearts of little beasties

The moon was dark   1

Ebony dark

Ringed like Saturn

With a glow of light

The spirits grew bold

And came forth

To roam between the worlds

Mouse could see them
As they danced and fought

He could hear the worms
Complaining to the Mother
With their full-hearted songs
Sometimes She would listen
And send the wind
To blow the spirits to the
mountains
And the trees would breathe a
sigh
And relief

Would rustle through their leaves
Like a spring blessing

And mouse would dance a little jig
Very softly   of course
So as not to disturb the beautiful
worms

But just enough
To show a gladness
To the always radiant Mother

The beetle was happy   2
Rolling his dung balls
Up the hill
To his small home
He liked the work
Making dung into balls
Especially he liked
Rolling it away
Sometimes he worried
That his life was too repetitive
The same thing
Over and over and over
But then

He would stop

And listen to the song of life

All around him

He would have enjoyed

Being a song beetle

Instead of a dung beetle

But his mother would always say

There is no higher work

Then making balls from dung

Be happy

Doing the work

You were born to do

Your talent

Makes the Mother happy
And it is always good
To make the Mother happy
So, the beetle
Just hummed to himself
And rolled his balls
Up the hill

The spider and the frog   3
Walked together down the log
They had been friends for a very
long time

There were no poets to tell their
story

And who would ever believe it

anyway

If there were

It mattered not to them

The spider would hunt for them
both

And the frog would stand guard

Over his dear old friend

And happily, clean up the
leftovers

And so, it was

In a million years

They would be lovers

So deep was their bond

The frog would be a prince of
thieves and the spider

His beautiful and dangerous
bride

And songs would be sung

And poems would be written

But their love would only

Grow brighter and deeper   and
true

But who would ever believe it

Besides the small mouse

Who knew them both Very well

Run Run   squeaked the mouse

The Snake is coming the Snake

is coming

And he is hungry for love

Relax, said the Mulla

He will not eat you

Not today anyway

He only wants to hold you in his

coils

And sing

Well , so you say said the mouse

So, you say

But we all know

That you will say anything

When you have drunk enough

wine

Not ever!   said the Mulla

Only slightly offended

When I drink the wine

I only speak the truth

Yes   yes   so you say
But how can I trust a drunken
Mulla

Well, said the Mulla
How can you not?
I am after all   a holy man

Throughout history, said the
mouse
It is the holy men that have
caused
All the trouble

And then
You blame it all   on God

Well, said the Mulla
Who else can you blame for
everything

5

The mouse was very careful
It was a full moon after all

The lotus pond was hungry for
reflection

And beauty   was in the air

It is the perfect soup   to feed a
hungry mouse

Who is yearning to be seen

And full of love

(To Albert, with love)   6

The Bear was old

But still very strong

With bears

True strength never leaves

He was no longer concerned

With the idiocy of the world
around him

For a moment

His spirit roused up

One of his family was in trouble

He stretched out a formidable
paw

Filled with love   and invincibility

The freedom bell rang out

And all those he loved

Were very glad to be loved

By such a Bear as he

7

The mouse was thinking

As he sat upon his favorite log

He was thinking about shadows

How they always pretended to be
still

And yet the moment you turned
your back

They would leap and dance

And cause all manner of trouble

And yet

No one ever saw them, but mouse

He saw them

And they laughed at him

And did outrageous things

Just to provoke him

He complained about this

To his friend   the dung beetle

Who also only laughed at him

The spider and the frog

Were always too busy hunting

To be bothered

By his philosophical quandaries

It was only snake

That even paid the least attention

To this topic

Well of course, said the snake
The shadow world is actually
more real
Then this world
If you can see the big picture

And I rely on the shadows
To help me hunt
They hide me in the shadow land
When I need to be invisible
And they show me where to look

When I am hunting
You are lucky
If they let you see them
It means you are a shadow
watcher

And that is very rare!

Mouse felt rare and special for a
moment
But then he noticed
How the shadows laughed at him
And seemed to just ignore him
Most of the time

Then, he saw his own shadow

watching him

And smiling

So, he just smiled back

And then his shadow moved

Like he was dancing

And so, mouse, copied him exactly

And moved like his shadows,
shadow

And now his shadow laughed

And danced some more

Mouse suddenly understood

He was his shadows
Shadow dancer
And the door to the shadow land
Opened to him, And so
he decided to go and have a look
around

The doorway into the shadow
world was like a tunnel.

Dark and narrow it seemed, but
when he emerged out the other

side, it was all too bright, way
too bright.

He needed to shield his eyes in
order to see.

Then, he noticed, when his eyes
were shut, he could clearly see the
luminous beings all around him,
like figures of dancing starlight

But they were way to bright for
him to see with his eyes open.

When he finally opened his eyes
and looked away, against the
mountain, he could see shadows
cast by the dancing starlight
figures.

The shadows were all still.

He could even see his own
shadow, but it was not still.

It was dancing, even though he
was not moving at all.

He considered all this deeply,
and then he closed his eyes.

He saw himself as a starlight
dancer, and leaped into the air,

and then, suddenly, he could feel
himself as a shadow, upon the
wall of the mountain.

He felt his darkness and his
stillness,

But then, in the meadow, he saw
with his eyes closed,
his dancing starlight self.

It was like a poem he had written
but didn't quite remember.

And then he saw the tunnel move
like a darkness

Into a halo of light.

He knew that the moment was
upon him, so he ran for the tunnel
with all his strength.

And then he was back, in his life,
and he was outside

And he could open his eyes now
and see the world

When from his normal life, he
looked at his shadow again, it
bowed to him, and it was suddenly
ringed with light. Like a halo

And then, he could feel a dance
coming from deep inside
And so, he did it as it came
And then his shadow laughed and
clapped
And now he understood.
At last,   he understood.
The shadow laughed some more

Snake was watching for that silly mouse, when he emerged from his hole. He saw that mouse had a small halo of light around him, and he was very curious.

"So, mouse," says he, "you seem different.

Did you make it to the shadow world Afterall?"

Mouse stopped and looked hard at snake. He had a rainbow of colored light around his head.

Well, said mouse, I guess I did,
but it was very different from
anything I could ever have
imagined, and now, I can barely
remember it at all.

But you seem different to me now
snake, I can now see your
rainbow.   So, what is that
about?

The snake seemed to blush, and
the rainbow got brighter.

Well, I don't know but I think your eyes have changed.

I seem just myself to me, but you seem definitely brighter, which for a mouse, I am not sure is such a good idea.

The mouse laughed, and then he realized that snake was probably right. I wonder if I will glow in the dark, or grow brighter in the light, said the mouse.

The snake laughed; I think you
are going to need a bodyguard.
He said. Come back in the
evening, and we will talk some
more.

  And so began the legendary and
wonderous adventures of the snake
and the mouse, which went on for
a very long time, and which
became a story in its own right.

    But for right now, the
mouse realized he had a serious
problem. He needed a large

cloak, and a bodyguard,
immediately.

And as fate would have it, that's
exactly what was delivered to his
doorstep.

The end

Notes from the diary of dawn

The shadow hides the bounty of

light.

That connects all beings

Without the shadow

There is only One

Without limits

To be the one within limits

Is to uphold the world

And the diversity of creation

This is the soul

The One, within limits

Let US   NoW

Return to poetry

This is a book of poetry

Afterall

In fond remembrance   of
Dylan Thomas

It is my seventy fourth year to heaven

And glad birds fly

The crows have come

And all the small creatures of the forest

Raise a paw, or a foot, or a claw

To herald in my day

With a blessing

All around me is heaven

Before me and above me
The blue wilderness unfurls
Its Gandarva wings

I step up, and greet the day
Hallelujah is my song
Hallelujah is my way

It is a hallelujah day that
blossoms
With a fragrance of roses
And icy clear water

High mountains call down
That I may rise up

My wings have hardly been used
They are still strong
And so,   I fly-
Up and over   up and over and
Up and over every obstacle
In my way

Victory is my name
Victory is my game

Let all who know me
Hear the sound of victory

It is the final trumpet call
It is the last train coming

I will ride the victory rail
To the very end   of time

The eye

The eye is formed

Upon a moment of luminosity

Borrowed from the Sun

Once burning within you

It will forever burn

And so, begins the journey

Started from a spark

Awakened by light

It is a forever song we sing

Now and forever

That is our way
To know this truly
Is the gift

Nanda Devi

Wind crystals cling
To the sheer green
Great walls of the cliff
That falls forever
Into the last crevasse

That still breathes

In the deep bosom of the
mountain

That is the mother of the
Ganges

Nanda Devi

Bright is the solar wind

That sings her name

Bright is her light

That moves upon the waters

That heal the world

Jaya deva   jaya Ma   jaya
jaya Ganga Ma

Blessings

How do the blessings flow

Like a wind, oft the ocean

Or a prayer from the heart

Do they follow a line

From the mind

What is it that connects

The one   to the other

Always   God

Mind to mind

Heart to heart

The separation is always Maya

The connection is always God

Rose wind

The Rose wind knows

The bees will only draw the purest nectar

And the dawn swallow

Only drinks the purest dew

From each moment

A pure sublime is always present

It is God's sweet draught of life

And all for free

More golden

Then the lust of sweet desire

Or the kiss of tantric bliss

Returned

It is the final word

In the last poem

And it will stand in truth **forever**

I remember you

Basil nut root   buried deep
Red as ochre

Its fingers stretch for rubies
Growing silently and bright

It is this yearning for eternity
That drives the day

Always near
But never close enough

Ocean passes overhead

Its waves of push and pull

Define the moment

How I do miss

That wild blown sea

That always smells of God

It calls my name

And then   I remember you

There is a glad moment

There is a glad moment
When the golden wind
Moves you deep
Into the inner current
That place
In the river of time
Outside time's grasp
It is the real
That runs through the center
Of our heart
Everything stops there

When we stand in that golden
room

All the folly and the pettiness

Falls away

Loves deepest yearning

Is now revealed

Oh, what would we have done

For love's promise

Had we only known

It was real

Oh, what would we have done

Had we only known

We could not fail

Now talking God

Now talking God
With your feet I walk
With your limbs, I stride
With your body, I carry forth
For me, your mind thinks
For me, your voice speaks
For me, your senses reveal the
world
Beauty is before me, Beauty is
behind me
Above and below me, hovers the
beautiful

I am surrounded by it I am
immersed in it

In my youth, I am witness to it

And in old age

I walk serenely the beautiful trail

(This is a new version of an old
Navaho song)

The moment of the small

It is the moment of the small

I bow solemnly before

I touch its foot

I am ashamed

I can offer only   my beingness

A shadow   among wings

A simpleton   in despair

To believe

I offer everything

I will even feed the flies

My eyes

I lie among the stinging serpents

And cry

Ashamed of my

Unquenchable and irreverent

laughter

What can I say

It is the moment of the small

There is no more

I touch its toe

I giggle hopelessly

My death is not impressed

The Rose

The rose
Entwines the day
For love
With a fragrance
That evokes the soul

Flowers of innocence
Reveal the world

The orange blossom

Let us consider the orange blossom

Now that we are old

It is brief

And fragrant

And bold

It yearns only to

Enrapture a bee

Like me

For I am its lover

Foretold

Myself

Before I was myself

I was myself

Now this is strange

But true

I am contained within

That which I have always been

And more than this

Yet to be discovered

I am

The crackle

Let us consider now, the crackle

That comes when greatness

Breaks out its shell

And shines

In brilliant symphony

Upon delusion

It snaps   and rushes out

In flame   and jubilation

For joy is born

And truth

Can claim it's victory

At last

Let us be now

Let us be now
There, is moving too fast
Or being very still
Only the mind is running
Out of time

And within times grasp

And where shall we be now
Only here   is safe
Only here   is real

Everything else

Is the poor man's ride

To hell and back again

Sure, is a lot of trouble

For some blood   and some
delusion

Better to just sit down   and see
what happens

And now at last

We have come to a zero point

It is that place where more
understanding is required

In order to fully grasp   the moment

This is the point, where we need to
restart our understanding of

death.

Strangely enough, this is always the
zero point.

At the end of the twelfth century, in India, there lived a great Baba. His name was Jnanishwara.

By the time he was 20, he had already achieved the highest form of yoga. He was also deeply enlightened as well as fully embodied . This is always a very rare event.

By some astounding quirk of luck, his teachings have been preserved.

His older brother , who was also a saint, used to bring him down to the village for songs and prayers.

Since no one spoke Sanskrit in those days except the priests, the great holy books were unreadable by the common man.

The language spoken in those days was Marathi.

So, he would take two lines from the Bhagava Gita and translate the Sanskrit into marathi, and then he would explain the meaning.

As he was also the greatest poet in 900 years, his translations were both breath taking and beautiful. His brother wrote down his words, and it became a two-volume set known as The Jnanishswara.

My old guru, Yogishwar Muni, used to say, that if he could take only 2 books, in all the world, and be stranded on a desert Island, he would choose

The Jnanishwara.

Remember now, that the Gita is the fundamental guide to life, and yoga and transformation, in all Indian literature.   Probably one of the most important works in the Vedic tradition.

It is a part of the Mahabarata, which is a twelve-volume set and probably the most significant epic in the history of India.

William Buck's retelling of the Ramayana, and the Mahabarata make them extremely readable to the western mind.

I enthusiastically recommend them to you. But as far as understanding the Gita goes, you will never find a more poetic and lucid rendition then that of Jnanishwara.

 It is so rare to have a window into such a deeply enlightened being. His commentary on death is extraordinary and amazing.

I have taken a few passages from this work which perhaps will shed for you a new light on the understanding of death. Especially in light of my strange experiences with the insect world. I offer it to you for your own deeper consideration.

From   The Jnanaishwara

"if a pot be submerged in water, and is filled with water as well as immersed in it, then, should the pot be broken, would the water itself also be broken

Likewise, this outward form perishes, but the Self which exists without it continues. When reason grasps this knowledge, how can it be disturbed."

"Therefore, those who know Me at the hour of Death, give up their bodies and become one with me."

These are words we all like to hear, and probably already believe in, in one form or another. However, He continues.................

"Of whatever state (of being) he is thinking of, when at the end he gives up his body, That he attains to , being ever absorbed in the thought thereof."

"Usually when Death strikes in the breast, a man becomes that which his heart remembers at the final moment."

"Whatever comes before his mind at the moment of Death, he cannot avoid becoming one with it.

In the same way, whatever desires a man forms while he is awake, he sees as soon as his eyes are closed.

The longings that a man feels when alive, which remain fixed in his heart, come to his mind at the moment of Death.

Whatever he remembers at the time of
Death, he will attain that state.

Therefor, remember Me at all times."

"Similarly, with practice, keep
constantly before thy mind the highest
Being, then let the body live, or die."

He goes on with great detail and
precision, about the entire process.
The point that I am bringing to your
attention, is

the form you next take, is dependent
entirely on you.

You always get what you need, not what you want.

Bob Dylan wrote a song about this.

It's all about what you need for your own evolution into higher consciousness.

It has nothing whatever to do with reward, or punishment. Although, your last life will affect the outcome a lot.

We all carry our own heaven and our own hell, within our own minds, already.

195

In the **Gospel of Thomas**, another text hard to find,

Jesus makes the following statement.

"**Seek me not** in buildings of wood and stone.

For the kingdom of heaven is above you and below you, and all around you.

Lift the stone, and there you will find me, split the root, and there will I be.

He soever who know this, will find eternal life."

Meher Baba, one of the great avatars of this age, went into great detail about the evolution of the soul.

He made the point, that we all start at ground zero and slowly work our way up to a human form.

From mineral and plant to insect and worm, to bird and beast, until finally we achieve the highest form, which is the human form.

However, keeping this form is not so easy. In the Buddhist tradition, it is very hard to get a human body.

You must have lived very carefully to attain to it. And once you do, it is easy to lose it again.

197

Even in the highest levels of the subtle realm, when you have achieved all power and mastery over the physical world, if you go too far, you can find yourself as a cockroach , and starting at the beginning one more time.

Once you attain to the fifth level of the subtle realm, according to Meher Baba, only then is it permanent.

If you are a zealot, or a fundamentalist, then none of this will make any sense to you. Of course, you may find yourself waking up as a dung beetle, and then I suspect, it will.

The real point of all this is

What you are guaranteed in life, is an eternal soul, and within that soul lies you.

What form or body you may find yourself in, is not at all guaranteed.

You will get the body you need for your own particular journey towards higher being.

We are all going home in the end, how long that may take, makes no difference at all.

What religion we may practice, makes no difference . It is only how we live, not what we believe.

Meher Baba made the statement, that

"God cannot be talked about, or argued about, or written about in any way.

God can only be lived."

What I am recommending to you based, on my very fortunate experience as a shaman, is to cultivate an attitude of gratitude and acceptance towards everything.

Especially the practice of Suspending Judgement. This, as the Dali Lama has said, is the true meaning of love.

In my experience, all manifest form

have consciousness.

Otherwise, it would not have a form at

all.

 All consciousness can be touched by

another consciousness.

 This relationship is the fundamental

driving force of manifest creation.

 Learning to have a conversation

with everything and anything, well,

that's where all the fun comes from.

 Otherwise, you are just another

zombie with expensive glasses

 driving a fast car and seeing nothing

of the real world at all.

So where does it start?

It starts with reverence for all life.

It starts with a deep sense of the
equality of all life and all things.

In a famous scene from Carlos
Castaneda's work, The Journey to
Ixtland , Carlos finds himself lying on
his back, and talking to a beetle.

At that moment, the equality of all life
became a reality to him. He was no
different from the beetle. They were of
equal importance, in the eyes of Truth.

The Sun shines on everything the same, regardless of form.

Neem Karoli Baba, once made the comment that if a man desires a mango at the moment of death, he would be born again as an insect.

Which brings me to my next chapter.

Conversations I have had.

The very first real conversation I ever had in my life, was with **fire.**

I was five years old and living in North Caroline in the deep woods, next to the marine base in cherry point.

The squadron had all just finished building their own homes,

and I was standing in my back yard, watching my neighbor, a four-year-old boy, gleefully striking matches and throwing them into the tall grass that ran all the way to the creek, about 100 feet away.

I was very concerned about this obvious abuse of power, and yet, I was also fascinated.

Sure enough, it took about five minutes for the grass to catch and suddenly **Voom.** A wave of fire rose up and ran for the tall pine trees beside the creek.

I was to surprised to even be afraid. The woods were very dry, and the trees all immediately went up in flames,

within minutes, there was a wall of fire over 100 feet tall staring down at me.

I could only look up and marvel. Already the heat was intense, and the fire was raging.

As I gazed up at the great wall of fire, it seemed to me , obviously to be a living fire,

I could make out a face looking down at me. The whole event was so wonderous and exciting, I had no idea what to do.

As I gazed up at the fire, and he gazed back, suddenly he just whispered to me.   He said, "call the wind boy, call the wind."

Just instinctively I raised up my arms, and I called the wind, as I had always done when I would get lost in the woods.

In a flash, a strong gust of wind came from behind me, and the fire was blown back away from the houses, and into the woods.

I was filled with shock and awe,
and a deep gratitude for the fire
spirit who had just told me what
to do.

I already had a relationship with
the wind, but I never had one with
fire before. That was a
memorable first for me.

Of course, the troops arrived
shortly thereafter, along with bull
dozers and a lot of commotion . It
was all very exciting, but the
memory that has stayed with me,
is of my conversation with the
Fire, and the grace of the wind .

My next major encounter with fire come about forty years later.

I was living with my family in an old stone farmhouse , high in the mountains of northern New Mexico, in an area called Pacheco canyon.

It had been very dry for weeks. Quite unexpectedly a lightening fire took hold of the forest just over the mountain from us.

Within no time at all, it was blazing and out of control.

My son and I were standing in our back yard, looking up at the mountain and all the smoke pouring over it towards us.

The fire was definitely coming in our direction, and I was wondering how I could possibly save the house.

Just then a huge wall of fire broke over the top of the mountain. Once again, I found myself gazing up a this immense and magnificent being, as it just stood there and looked down on us.

I figured we had maybe fifteen minutes to get out of there.

I did not like the idea of running. I told my son to stand next to me and make contact with the fire being, then I said now, we must call the wind.

 So, we raised our arms and asked for the blessing of the fire, and we called the wind.

Fortunately for me, my son also had shamans' blood, and had called the wind many times as a boy on Maui.

It had never been so extreme however, and he had long forgotten about those very early days of his life.

Nevertheless, he dutifully stood at my side and did his best .

I just prayed and chanted and did everything I knew how to do.

After about five minutes,

I sensed the great wall of fire, stir,
and give a chuckle,

and sure enough, the wind
arrived and blew the fire back
down the mountain.

It continued to head away from us
for the rest of the day.

Once again, we were saved by the
wind. But that chuckle,

from a great wall of fire, I have
never forgotten.

The Wind

I have always felt a deep affection and love for the wind. From my earlies days. He was the father that was with me when I needed one.   She was the mother when I needed her.

He was the holding ground for my essential self.

My other father was ablaze in a life of being an elite corsair fighter pilot, in a squadron of Marines, who were all veterans and experienced in combat.

The problem, the real problem for all the men, was the fact that a squadron is a unit,

It must fly as a unite in precise and strange ways, which only long experience of flying with that unit will give you.

So, the bottom line was   " if you leave, then good chance it means the death of one of us, while the rookie is learning how to fly with us. "

"But hey, no pressure"

Of course, it was different in a non-combat zone. But in actual combat, that was just a reality.

None of this I ever knew or understood, until I was old, of course.

213

But somehow it all balanced out
in just the right way.

My father and the wind were
riding on the same horse and
living in the same house.

When I first consider the wind, I
remember immediately the fun of
the wind .

The sheer joy of learning how to
ride on the wind.

I would go out in the 80 mph
winds, known as the Santa
anna's, and climb up on tall
eucalyptus.

Probably the most dangerous tree
possible to go up in, because they
shatter when they break.

But I knew nothing except they seemed to bend enough. So, I would go high up and just blow in the wildness of the moment.

Then, if I was able to work it out, I would go down to the Warf, in the lagoon, where the sea explorers kept their boats.

Being one myself, I had access to the canoes.

So, then I would row out in the lagoon and putting my back and arms out, I would catch a wave of wind and just steer my canoe as straight as I could

And go across the lagoon. It was very invigorating

And an amazingly fast ride.

215

Of course, you had to wait awhile before you could row back. And there was no room for error in this game.

If I had tipped over in the wind, that would be a lot of trouble and put the end to my adventure, for good.

It was always a challenge, but of the most delicious kind.

I find that my memories are very rich and as deeply exciting to me now, as the experiences were then.

What a treasure.

Although my childhood is filled with the delight of this, the real adventure came from my time on Maui, and my relationship with an actual Thunder Being.

Perhaps, more appropriately called a Chen Lunn.

I discovered this amazing being early on in my exploration of the crater, Mt Haleakala.

This is a ten-thousand-foot volcano, which is still active, but that is a well-kept secret.

The tourist buses go to the top every morning, and the tourists can go walking down **sliding sands trail**, which is 30 plus miles of trails in a very lunar landscape.

There is a parking lot at the 8,000 ft level. Very few people, only the locals go there.

I could hike out from there just 20 minutes to the edge of the creator.

This was the very lush part of the creator. No lunar landscape.

I would go out on a small hill at the beginning of the trail and do my incense and offerings and singing and whatever was appropriate to the moment.

I noticed right away a very shapely bank of clouds, resting easily on the opposite side of the crater, just nestled in.

It was thirty miles across.

Very gradually, as I kept my eyes upon it, the absolute image of a perfect dragon's head, in all its glorious and fine detail, slowly rose up out of the bank.

I was stunned. I gazed into its eyes and gave a song, just spontaneously .

Well, that was the beginning.

It turns out that this being was in fact, the real deal.

There was a bright kind of intelligence, but more of a curiosity to relate with a human being again.

As I am sure the kahunas had done for centuries before me.

Now, it turns out that I had a unique need for cloud cover, in order to go to my secret cave, which was in plain view, right at the bottom of the trail.

Whenever I would go out on the mountain, he would always appear.

So, I began to cultivate a real relationship with him.

I would make many offerings
of food and spiritual substance,
and lots of music and chanting.

 But mainly I just enjoyed being
with him.

And when I would go down the
trail, he would always come and
give me cover. Every time.   He
did not miss one time in 20 years.

One time he just came over
when I was playing my flute and
he covered me with a golden
sparkle, and what that did to my
soul, I cannot describe.

It had a deep brightness to it,
and a lot of profoundly good
feelings.

He could cover the distance between us in less than a minute. Suddenly he would just be there.

He was an immensity of cloud, but his head was always defined and clear.

There was a lot of genuine affection between us.

The event however that I am now referring to happened later in our relationship.

The Hurricane

I had just pulled into my driveway listening to the radio, and there was a storm with 100

mph winds headed to the creator.
I was very glad to be home.

Suddenly I was told in no
uncertain terms, by my old friend,
to get to my cave immediately,
and to do it now.

I had a moment of shocked
disbelief and just sat in my truck.

Then I was told to go now, or it
would be never.

The finality of that never, just did
not feel right.

So

I moved into high gear and
grabbed my pack and my bag and

my stick ,Fred , and drove as fast as I could back up the mountain.

I was sure the gate would be closed, but I knew I had to give it my best shot. When I reached the gate, it was open in order to get all the cars out. I arrived at the perfect moment when the guard was busy, and I just slipped through and got to my parking lot unseen.

I jumped from my truck and ran down the mountain three miles, to my cave. I could feel the electricity in the air and the wind was already intense.

My first thought was to go to shelter in the back of my cave, but

100 mph winds are going to find you, wherever you are.

 I understood that the situation was not about survival.

So, I just walked out into the day and the sun was just setting. I took my position and looked up at the thunder beings all around me.

Suddenly a 60-mph blast of freezing cold air just hit me in the chest. I crumpled like a dog.

But I knew my only chance was to get up and just sing my heart out. So that is what I did.

My prayers were always
contact driven and revealing of
my heart. I would always include
a prayer to become more useful. I
kept it up nonstop and watched
the Chen Lun above me.

The first was golden light, as
the Sun was just going down. It
was filled with a joy and
confidence, and a love of the
truth. It was like gold itself.

Slowly he rose up, and then
slowly back down.

Then another immensity of red
and gold rose up.

The red was bright and brave and
strong. It was filled with courage
and passion. It is beyond words
to describe.

Then he rose up and then down
and then another very dark
dragon rose up.

 He was not solid black, but dark
and with lightening flashes.
There was a wildness and a power
there that I cannot began to
describe.

    Then he rose up and down, and
then there was a pause.

I felt relieved. Like I had survived
the ordeal.

Then another dragon rose up,

   5 times as big and full of
thunder and blackness.

He looked at me with a ferocious
eye, from which I felt little
compassion.

   He said, "you have five
minutes,"

His contact was brief and terrible.
I howled for my life and danced
like a fool.

   Then he stopped me and simply
said ok," now you may go. You
have 45 minutes to get back to
your car before I will come for
you."

I flew back to the cave, and grabbed my stuff, and ran for my life. I had about a quarter of a mile of ahh ahh stone to cross before I would hit the trail. Very dangerous footing.

Then it was 3 miles up a very steep switch back trail to the top, and then a 10 min run to the parking lot.

I looked at my watch and got my mark, and then I just let my spirit go wild and moved like an animal.

Finally, I got to my truck, opened the door and slammed it shut. I was immediately hit by a gust of wind that almost blew me over.

I checked my watch. It was exactly 45 minutes. I had just made an impossible run.

Fortunately, there was still someone there at the gate, and I drove out as quick as I could go.

When I reached my house at the four-thousand-foot level, the wind was greatly lessened.

It was raging inside the crater, but outside it was just windy. I collapsed on my bed, grateful to still be alive.

The true depth of that experience has taken me a lifetime to understand.

The water

As with the wind, many stories could be told.

My experience of water began in earnest when I became a junior in high school.

Somehow, I ended up joining the swimming team, which was run by an insane coach. He was the PE teacher, as well as the swimming coach.

After school, he would take the team to a private pool, which was very warm. It was very hard to swim races in a hot pool. That was the idea.

We had to swim five miles, just for a warmup, and that was

timed. If you didn't beat the
clock, you had to do two, 200-
yard butterflies for time. It was
truly brutal .

   The result of all this was, I
could swim two and a half lengths
of the Olympic pool under water.
I could hold my breath for over 4
minutes. I was not a great speed
swimmer, But I was a tireless
swimmer.

When I reached the oceans of
Maui, I was ready.

The very first thing I did was buy
my diving rig. I only did free
diving without tanks mostly, but I

got the very best mask and
snorkel, the very best large fins,
and a beautiful 6-foot-long sling
spear and gloves, and a knife.

Every day for almost a year and a
half, I would walk down to the
ocean and teach myself to dive. It
was a long slow process.

 It was surprisingly hard to really
learn your way around in the
ocean. Very different from a lake
or a river.

  In the real ocean, where there
are few boats or people, big fish
live.   They could appear at any
time, but if they did, it was just
you and them. There was no
safety net.

There were monster rip tides and currents, and lots of wind and waves. It was not an easy place to hang out in for to long, especially when the weather was up.

If you ever got caught in one of the express currents, you were in for a very long ride to a very hard place.

The coast of Molokai , where you would end up is only monster waves and rocks.

So, there was every good reason to know what you were doing, before you did it.

It took me about a year, as I was already a very strong swimmer.

But there was a lot to be learned about tides and currents and moving in the deep water.

About how to swim underwater most efficiently. About how to keep a 360-degree vigilance at all times.

There was a lot to understand about the ocean.

After a while, I learned. And then I would tie my net and spear to a small bogey board, which had a rope that I would then tie to the bottom .

The reef was almost a mile out in the open sea. The depth was only 30 to 50 feet for about 3 miles before you would hit the channel. Then it would drop to hundreds and even thousands.

The side I dove on was the leeward side, and it was a milder ocean. The windward side was much wilder, much sooner, and a lot bigger critters swam there.

On this side, there were a lot of bad currents and wind in the afternoon, but it was a safer place most of the time.

On this particular day, it started out beautiful and sunny and calm, but then the wind came.

Soon it was very rough and choppy, and a lot of bad currents were forming.

I did not really pay to much attention to the coast, as there were a lot of fish suddenly all around me.

By the time I looked up and tried to find my mark, I realized I had drifted miles further down into the bad currents and rough water.

Not only that ,but I had also drifted away from my board and now the waves were too high for me to see over them.

So, I lost my board, my net and my spear, and I was far, far out in the bad water.

 I started to swim back on the surface, but it was exhausting. The wind and the currents were brutal.

   And then, I remembered my Charlemagne, as Indiana Jones father famously said. Suddenly I knew, the only way to go, was to go deep.

   I dove down to about 30 feet, and suddenly everything was very calm. No wind, no waves, no bad currents. I just cruised along in perfect equanimity.

Fortunately, I could hold my breath for a very long time. After two hours or so of going along on the bottom, surfacing only to breath, I rose up and took my bearings.

 I had almost made it back to my mark on the coast where the road to my home began.

I was saved by going deep and just completely relaxing my mind. I learned a lot from that experience.

If I had not done that, I would have most certainly been drowned like a rat.

 That lesson saved me a lot of pain and trouble in my life to come.

The gauntlet

In our ever-expanding search for new sea caves and wild bits of coast, Patrick and I, discovered a totally deserted and extremely formidable stretch of the coast just above Davenport, calif. We found it quite by accident as we were walking along the beach.

All of a sudden, we found ourselves in a very rugged bit of cliff and rock with deep crevasses. We made our way through the obstacles until we came to a large sandstone and gravel rock cliff that rose up in front of us.

The cliff jutted way out into the ocean, with a huge waterfall coming down off one wall, nearest the beach, and a large hole in the ocean side with the tide blasting through. It was steep and probably over 200 feet tall. It was quite mythic.

We both felt like we had just been transported to Hawaii. We tried to climb up slowly in the traditional manner, but only succeeded in sliding down on the very loose gravel.

I noticed that there were a few fixed and very large rocks that could be used as a ladder, if you had enough forward momentum.

So, feeling the wild thrill of the moment, I ran hard for the cliff and managed to scratch my way up to the first fixed rock.

I was able then, to keep my momentum up and go for the next bolder. So little by little I was able to make it to the top, without sliding back down.

Now this was a rare moment for me. It was the first time I had done something that Patrick was not able to do. He had already tried twice and failed twice. But seeing me sitting at the top and laughing

Was just too much for him.

He threw himself into an Irish rage and ran for the cliff with all his might.

Luckily, I was able to reach out and grab his hand, before he slid back down again, when he neared the top.

We had miraculously made it up, but now getting down the back side was the problem. We paused and looked out upon a scene of wonder.

The cliff dropped down onto a sheet of flat black basaltic stone.

It extended for hundreds of feet along the coast and was covered with millions of small black crabs who would all scurry out when the water receded.

Beautiful but small, and very perfect crystalline waves would flow in from the ocean to give it light and fury.

It was a beautiful and amazing sight, but the getting down part was going to be a problem.

We could climb down about halfway to a ledge, but then the only way down was to just drop about 15 feet to the bottom.

Once you were down, there was no way back up. That was the primary characteristic of the gauntlet. You could go forward, but you could not go back.

So down we went, trusting in our luck to get us home again . Every cove we came to was different, and every cove had its unique challenges.

At the end, before you came out on a gentle beach again, there

245

was a 200-yard section of beach up against the cliffs.

At low tide, the beach was only four feet wide, and you had to time your run perfectly to make it before the next very large wave would smash against the wall.

It was quite exciting and difficult to manage without getting crushed by a wave.

On this particular occasion, which was to be our last time, we had deeply miscalculated the tides.

When we got to the last beach, the tide was already in and the water was too deep to swim across or wade across next to the cliffs.

The waves were huge and very strong.

We were completely screwed.

Our only hope was to wait for a boat to come along, which we knew very well was not going to happen in our lifetime.

So, I walked out to the end of the rocky bluff, which extended about 200 feet out into the sea.

Watching the large waves come in I realized that if we timed it just right, we might be able to swim across.

But the ocean seemed quite formidable and wild and unpredictable.

There was a lot of white water and heavy currents and general chaos . It appeared like an impossible swim into madness.

Patrick, was not a very strong swimmer and to him, it seemed far too dangerous.

I , on the other hand, was a very strong swimmer with a lot of experience with waves and tides.

Also, I realized there was no other choice .

So, I informed Patrick, that if he followed me very closely and precisely, with perfect timing, he might survive the day. .

He realized also that there was no other choice.

So, I waited for a smaller set of waves to go by, and then I leaped in behind the last wave and began to swim furiously away from the beach.

Patrick, to his credit kept close enough to me and we managed to get out far enough to ride over the top of the next large wave coming in.

So now we just had to stay far enough out to not be pulled in by any wave, and we slowly made out way across, through all the foam and madness.

It appeared impossible when you looked at it from above, but when you were in it, you realized it was all rage and fury, signifying nothing.

Another lesson, deeply imprinted
upon my soul .

The last bit was difficult. We had
to wait for the perfect wave, and
then ride up on the back of it and
grab onto the cliff just high
enough too be able to hold on,
and not fall into the barnacles and
wild wash below.

By a bit of Irish luck, and cunning,
we managed to get on the cliff
and climb up and over to the
beach, and suddenly we were
back in civilization.

The beach was covered with the
young and the beautiful and
mostly naked.

250

We felt like we had just emerged from a war zone and found ourselves suddenly in heaven.

It was a study in illusion and timing and courage.

It was a lesson I truly needed to understand.

The life of a shaman is so much more than just being able to relate to all things. It is a profound introduction to the medicine wheel.

   You cannot help but see it . This teaching was kept secret for many years by the Native Americans.

I had the great good fortune to meet and to spend some time with Sun Bear.

Sun Bear was given the task of bringing it to the light of day. At the time he was an alcoholic veteran, living on the street and suddenly he was given the job.

He rose to the challenge and wrote two wonderful books as well as traveled and taught about the medicine wheel for the rest of his life.

What an impressive man he was. He confided in me some very personal stories of his life, before and after his revelation.

It was in fact an authentic revelation that came to him and literally dragged him out of the gutter and put him on the path of teaching about the wheel.

Much to the dismay of many Native Americans. He encountered great resistance, on his road to bringing forth the teaching.

To understand about the medicine wheel, is to understand about the interconnectedness of everything and to see your own life, always as a teaching, rather than as a form of accomplishment , or punishment.

Every day of your life reveals the pattern you are in, if only you have eyes to see, and ears to hear.

It is so much more than seeing the tea leaves at the bottom of your cup.

Once a deep reverence for life has awakened within your heart, and the equality of all life is now a living truth within your soul, then you can receive a teaching from anything, and anyone.

You know it is all Spirit, finding its way before you.

Your job is always to just have the humility to recognize how Spirit moves in everything, and to accept the truth it is always bringing before you.

What was the actual turning point for me was my chance meeting with a very large Siberian tiger, in the Olympic rain forest in Washington.   My life was forever changed, by that event.

254

The Tiger

I had been driving in a remote section of the road that wound around the park. I happened to notice a sign, off the road and near to a house. It said "wolves".

There was a trail that started going back into the forest, some ways from the house.

I decided to follow this trail first, just to have a look around.

I walked some ways into the forest that seemed totally deserted. I came around the corner and suddenly I was face to face with the largest tiger I had ever seen.

I was totally unprepared for that reality.

I noticed that he was contained, but only just barely.

He was in a small enclosure of very flimsy wire, which even a dog could have broken out of, if he was motivated.

It turns out it was only a very temporary enclosure for that day only, while his real cage was being prepared.

What defined the moment for me, however, was the fact that he was in full crouch, with his eyes fixed firmly upon me.

I realized immediately that the cage was no barrier at all, and he could easily walk through it if he wanted to, and he, I realized, could see that as well.

So, I was faced with a tiger in full crouch, and he was already moving closer to me, and he was only 15 feet away.

I immediately knew that running was not an option. I saw that he was completely wild and ready to have me in whatever way he wanted.

Fortunately for me, the moment was so extreme, that my mind just left the room. I understood that my only hope was to go with my shamanic instincts, which were completely

the opposite of what my mind
wanted to do.

So, I made eye contact with him
and crouched down and leaped
right at him.

He immediately did the same.
So, there we were, standing face
to face, and he was absolutely
huge.

He looked at me without giving
me any indication of what he was
going to do.

I knew the next move was on
me, so I pushed the barrier one
step closer.

I kept eye contact with him,
filled with a deep admiration, and
I carefully put my hand through
the wire and touched his face.

Well that genuinely surprised him, and he looked at me very carefully and very deeply. He decided to accept my challenge and take it to the next level.

Rather than just eat me on the spot, he gave me a long very intense contact and showed me the deeper side of Tiger.

He showed me that all tigers were connected, and they knew they were connected.

The strength of one, was really the strength of the many.

He showed me the deeper level of consciousness that he actually embodied.

The contact just went on and on, the depth of it, just went on and on.

I was deeply excited and thrilled.

What was transmitted to me, changed my life.

I cannot even begin to describe it. After about 20 minutes or so he decided to lighten the mood.

He showed me that he wanted to play.

I immediately began to pretend that I was rubbing his stomach.

He immediately turned over and rolled around in glee. This

went on for some time until we were finally interrupted by a Native American woman who was deeply disturbed by my presence so close to the tiger.

I told her that I would sign anything she wanted, but I wanted to go inside with the tiger.

She was horrified. She said the tiger was completely wild, they had only just received it that day.

The cage was only a very temporary situation, while they were getting his real cage ready.

She said that obviously I was a completely crazy white man, and I had to leave now.

261

The tiger seemed to fade back into his normal reality, and I slowly walked away, completely amazed and forever changed.

As we walked out, she told me how they had just received him.

He was over 900 lbs she said, which made him very rare. It was only because he was being fed so well, that they were able to keep him in the cage, at all.

The level of consciousness that he shared with me was completely off the charts. He seemed to have no animosity towards men, only a slight disdain.

Perhaps I was able to surprise him and show him that all humans were not complete idiots.

Some were actually able to relate, without fear and panic. Without guns and a safety net.

I feel like our time together came from the grace of another time, when we perhaps were both tigers.

He was like my long-lost brother. He was family, in some sort of strange way.

The details didn't seem to really matter. What mattered was the real connection that was between us. That's all that mattered.

263

After that moment, I had a new and deep reverence for all life.

I truly understood that all life was of equal value and importance.

I understood that man simply had his place on the medicine wheel. An equal place.

He was my first real experience of kingliness .

I understood then, what it was to be a real king .

I certainly had never meet one before in the human world that was even close to his level of consciousness and majesty.

Except for the Baba's , of course.

Let us move from the
sublime,

 To the mundane.

Often in my life, I discovered that
I would develop a connection with
things that were not living.

Or, at least, did not appear to be.

   The stone people, and the
crystal people, were the first that I
became fascinated by.

   It seems that I just couldn't help
picking up the stones or crystals
that moved me, and putting them
in some sort of an altar, or special
place. I would often dream of
them or find them in my dreams.

I was always deeply moved by them. It was probably for that reason that Charly Tom gave me his blessing to begin to give stone people lodge or sweat lodge as we call it today.

A Karoc medicine chief doesn't give instructions, in their tradition, if you want to know something, then you must just ask the Great Spirit.

He would only talk to me in stories. He told me many stories, mostly about the person we call Big Foot.

To this day I never really understood why those stories.

But I did get that I had to talk to the stone people if I wanted to use them for the ceremony.

266

Many of them would decline, but some would agree.

For them, it meant they would be heated to red hot, and then, water was put on them, to make the steam.

The steam would carry their song and their healing for the group of people who were there.

Often as a result of this, they would crack apart. So, it was no small matter for them.

I was always very careful to only chose the ones that wanted to come.

If you chose the wrong stone, it could explode, and kill people very easily. So great care had to be exercised in the choosing of stones.

The healing songs they would send through me were always surprising and interesting to me. The results especially. were always very enlightening.

I remember a beach on Maui, that was in a very remote section of the coast.

There was a sacred church, called the Aloha Church that was located there.   Many great and powerful old Hawaiians were buried around there.

I remember walking along the coast that went on for miles past the Church. It was all very large stones and boulders that rolled forever in the tide and the wash, as it came in and out.

 The sound haunts me still. It was a roar and a grinding of so many that moved in the water.

When I touched any of the stones, I would be filled with a memory of a distant time. Often, it was of very, very distant times. The things that I saw and felt seemed almost Atlantean.

Often the memories were filled with a great sadness. Fascinating as it was, the emotions were almost to much for me.

The emotions didn't seem to be so much in the stones, as my own reaction to them.

The memories filled me with strong emotion. For some reason, that particular stretch of coast was just full of history and was readily accessible. I didn't know what to make of it all really, and it soon wore me out.

I have often felt a deep connection to the stone people, but never was it so emotionally intense.

Charly Tom had one assistant, which he often used. Strangely enough he was a white man. I met him years later on Maui, when we were doing the Native American church, which is a peyote ceremony that is

long and somewhat taxing, as you had to remain sitting up all night.

I found the ceremony thrilling and difficult.

Afterwards, Bruce and I got to talking about Charly.

He informed me that Charly was indeed a true sorcerer, or powerful shaman. I had suspected as much.

He told me of the time he had complained to Charly about a friend of his , living in Canada, who was being threatened by the Nazis. Today of course, they go by the name of Alt Right, but only the name has changed.

So, the problem was that they were giving him death threats, and he was very worried. Charly asked ,if he had ever been to his

friend's apartment in person, and
Bruce answered that he had.

So then, they went to a special
place in the woods, and Charly
asked him to remember the apt.

Then he started to beat his
drum very loudly and huge
amounts of light were blasting out
of it. Suddenly, Bruce said, he
was actually standing in the
apartment.

He could only really see the
intense light all around him, and
then they were back in Calif
again.

He called his friend in Canada
several days later to check on
him.

    His friend said that it was the strangest thing, but all the Nazis had suddenly just disappeared.

 He had no explanation.

Bruce only smiled and shook his head.

    He then told me another story of the time Charly had sent him to the caldera of a large volcano.

Bruce said he was sitting down next to a huge cliff that looked distinctly like a human face. He had chosen that spot, for that very reason.

    He was thinking about what Charly had told him. How the stone people could talk to you if they wanted.

When suddenly, out of the blue, a very deep voice, a very loud voice began to speak to him. He said it was so loud, that it completely amazed him.

He just got up and walked away as fast as he could. He told me that holding a conversation with a giant stone cliff, was a very weird experience.

I have often seen those faces on mountains and many a cliff, but I have never had a conversation with one, not audibly at any rate.

Time to talk about Fred

I found Fred at the bottom of the second sacred pool, on Maui. This was a remote and truly astounding place on the coast, aptly named because of the seven sacred pools that were there.

On the one side, there were four pools that ran down to the sea. Large and deep. With waterfalls and a bridge, that locals would dive off , for money.

On the other side of the road, were the three large pools, with waterfalls and deep water. These were only accessible by walking. There was no easy access to them.

But the four lower pools were a big tourist attraction, and very dangerous in bad weather.

In bad weather, which means hard rains in the interior, huge amounts of water would then wash down the river and come to the pools in the form of a thirty-foot wall of water. Many people died, even with all the precautions.

It was my very first time on Maui. I managed to get to the pools, as I loved to dive in deep water, and these were spectacular to behold.

So , as I approached the second pool, I noticed that it was deeper than the first. Still narrow, but much deeper.

I barely made it down the seventy feet to the bottom.

I had no time to look around, but there was Fred, looking back at me.

So, I grabbed him and blasted for the top.

I have taken him with me on all my adventures ever since. He has saved my life many times . He is actually a Rooty, not just a stick and a companion.

He was made naturally from a piece of a root from a mango tree. Very strong, with the head of a goat. He is a goat root Rooty, and I love him.

Now, we enter into a different realm. The realm of objects, that have spirit, and have consciousness.

For most, that is a leap.

Not for the samurai, however. He knows the spirit that lives within his sword, and if he is true, then that spirit is true, and the sword is true.

It would not even be up for serious consideration.

Of course, the sword has a spirit.

If you are a medicine man or wizard with a staff,

Of course, the staff has a spirit.

And you probably know how to use it.

This is the realm, where in you must give your imagination free roam to always support the spirit rising, the vortex always is awash with rising spirits.

This is the moment where you must look and see the painfully obvious.

As a shaman, when I look at the world of stuff.   I don't see dead stuff.

I see only a living force . The base of this living force is pure awareness. When this pure awareness is rubbed and loved and comes under the eye of the beholder, then it responds, and in that response, becomes self-aware.

Self-awareness is the fundamental root of consciousness.

That is why everything works the way it does. We are dealing with a living force of being. In order to recognize this being, there must be love.

There is a dead realm for certain, but it is more of a hell realm, than any objective science. It is a realm of hopelessness and despair; it is not objective anything. It is where you go when you have given up.

Even in the dead land, there is hope. That is the beautiful part. As a shaman, I can see the hope rising off the meadows in whiffs and dawn light mists.

I can see the energy as it moves and rises.

I am not confused about the presence of Spirit in everything.

Sadly, many people are. I have seen where that confusion can lead.

I have seen the realm of the dead. It is no place I wish to hang about in, not for any reason.

But I am lucky, I have been given a true moment of union with Great Spirit.

Now, I no longer have any confusion. Now. I have sorrow, yes, but also great jubilation and joy. There is no more doubt and dead thinking.

 If you are truly wounded and full of hatred and rage, and deep loneliness. The hell realms will make you willing, so you can be healed. Everyone has a limit as to how much suffering they can endure.

Eventually you will find your limit.

Then you will open yourself up to love again. You will open yourself to healing. And the journey will begin again.

What is it to be truly alive?

  It is to feel the spirit within you, and around you and all about you. Once you have begun to open your subtle eyes and senses, the intensity of that aliveness will amaze you.

 You will no longer choose to go unconscious or asleep.

You will no longer wish to keep your eyes closed and just get high.

You will no longer choose the way of the rejector.

Now you will say   YES

It is a fundamental shift, to be sure. But it is a shift that everyone must make, if they want to leave the dead zone.

This is why people are drawn to the things that amplify their life.

Easy to get lost in that pleasure and delusion loop.

And boy, will you suffer for it.

But eventually you will be drawn to truth. And with that comes beauty and music and great art. That is the realm of joy.

Eventually you will be attracted there.

That is the very reason that all life moves in circles, instead of lines and points or dots.

When you find yourself moving in circles and sphere's,

Then you are rising into the
knowledge of the love of truth.

Which means that purity and love
must have somehow made their
way into your heart.

All this just to describe Fred?

We all know how we can get lost
in stuff.

 Every musician, if he is good, will
love and create a relationship
with his instrument.   The same
for a swordsman.   The same for
any craftsman with his tools .

    And how about all the holy
shrines we venerate and statues

we worship. The list just goes on and on with this.

We are always forming a relationship with our stuff.

The only real question is, how deep will we go with this.

When you finally and eventually come to the realization that everything and everyone is God.

Well, you can go deep, as deep as you dare.

That is basically the place you are standing in, if you are an authentic shaman.

I am trying to get back to you
Fred. I am trying.

Let me just finish up here .

The shamans heart starts out with

First, acknowledging the divine
within all others and all things.

Second, reaching out from his
heart, to form a relationship with
that which is the being, in
whatever form it may appear.

If order for this to work,

There must be openness and
suspension of judgement,

and authenticity in being one's
own true self.

That is why a real shaman can
have a relationship with anything,

and have it be authentic in the end, instead of a meaningless fantasy.

Its about keeping the value and integrity in your life, as well as the joy and the fun.

The sorcerer and the scientist are both seeking to understand, and control. Mainly, there, it is a search for power.

The shaman is not wanting to control anything, he is mainly seeking to keep the dance of spirit moving, that all may rise into the love of truth.

Very different end game.

He is seeking a relationship and an ally, for the affairs of his life. He is not seeking to manipulate and deceive and control, in order to get more power.

He is seeking to heal, if needed, and provide inspiration and real help. He is seeking real friendship. Not delusion.

So, how does Fred fit into all of this.

Well, a real adventure must be taken, in order to better understand Fred more fully.

I always knew that Fred was special.   I really did not know why in the beginning.

The first real adventure when Fred revealed more of himself, was

the search for the Hidden Valley'

The Search for the Hidden Valley was an adventure that Bruce and I had long dreamed of doing, and finally , one fine day we did.

Maui is truly an amazing place. It is full of the magical and the arcane.

Mt Haleakala is one of the twelve most sacred places in the world.   It is the ten-thousand-foot active volcano on the Island of Maui.

That is where I spent a lot of time with my friends. And that is where the adventure begins.

If you wish to find out about a friend, then you must have a real adventure with them, then you will find out what they are made of.

Most of my friends on Maui, could do a casual adventure, very well. But a real adventure, where your life may be at risk, and heroic strength and resolve may be needed to survive at all, then you must choose your friends very carefully.

On the mainland, I had Patrick. He was my true climbing partner, and I could trust him with my life.

On Maui, there was Bruce. Bruce was strong, stronger than me, and very rugged. He could keep up.

I knew I could rely upon Bruce for courage and fortitude; and to pull me out of a hole.

It is the fortitude part that everyone has trouble with.

I have found that in order to really survive anything, you must be able to find your heroic fortitude.

Heroic fortitude is a real asset in a climbing partner.

All my real adventures always demanded of me, the heroic.

That is the larger-than-life part, of just having a life. That is also the fun part, especially when it is over, and you have survived.

Every time Bruce and I crossed over to the crater at the eight-thousand-foot level, and went in the back way, we crossed over a small bridge, called the rainbow bridge.

293

It was so named by all the mist and rainbows that grew there.

When you crossed over into the crater, on a good day, you could see down into the valley that was about two thousand feet below the craters floor , which was three thousand feet below where you were then. So, five thousand feet below , we would get a tantalizing glimpse of the hidden valley.

We could see it was deeply lush and full of rainbows and magic. But, climbing down the cliffs right there would require a lot of rope and effort.

So, we dreamed and planned for the day.

294

The years past, and then we both felt the deep desire, once again.

So, we pulled together a very long day, ropes and climbing gear and food for the trek.

The plan was simple, just go down to the cliffs at the bottom of the crater and find a way to get down to the valley below.

The first valley that we went down, was very steep.

It appeared still possible , but very steep.

After a few hundred yards we came to a large crack in the very floor of the gulch and another that went down beside it. Walking very slowly down the vertical crack, I could just peer into another world.

The edge of the cliff had opened to reveal a deep bed of crystals that extended back about 40 feet or so. It was maybe 2 to 3 feet high. Just big enough for me to crawl into.

I, who grew up on treasure lore and fairy Stories of magic crystals gazed in with hungry eyes.

I had never seen a full bed of crystals , so perfect and so remote, and untouched, by any hand but mine.

As I gazed deeply into my treasure world, Bruce carefully

made his way past me to look further down the valley.

We had reached the end point of being able to go back up. If we went any further down, then we would be committed. Going back up would not be an option. We were both hoping to continue down, as the last 100 yards had been very steep. To go back up now, was possible, but only just.

Bruce was edging his way down, trying to get the long view, and I was lost in a wonder of treasure.

As I gazed deeper in, my eyes fell across a huge, bright green and astoundingly large crystal.

My fortune was made was my
first thought.

Then as I looked closer, I realized
that I would have to crawl over
and on top of, this magnificent
and very fragile bed of very
delicate crystals.

And who could even say the real
role that giant crystal played
within this world.

I realized that I would be
making enemies of some very
powerful crystal people if I just
busted them all to hell to crawl
over them to get the queen.

I longed to have her, but I
slowly began to understand the
real test I was facing here.

With great reluctance I pried my mental fingers from off the fairy queen and let her go.

I knew immediately that I had made the right decision. I felt relief, but also a deeper yearning to have her.

I understood that I would have to be content with the metaphysical, though I longed for the physical to be real at last.

Bruce returned with bad news. No way down, without a lot of rope.

So, up we went at a very steep scramble to get up and over the worst.

299

I was still filled with dreams of the magic queen, so I was distracted from the severity of the climb.

We got up finally and rested from the ordeal. But now the sun was out, and the day was getting warmer and moving on quickly.

We knew we had to move it along.

We came to the next valley that went down. It was all grass for the first 200 yards, and then went down steeply to join a large forest of ohia trees. The trees were about 30 ft tall and very dense and thick and hard to get over or around.

And then it seemed to go more gently down to the valley far below.

It seemed easier to us than the last valley, so we headed down.

What we had not realized, was how impossible it was to see , once we were deep in .

Fortunately, I spotted a red tie, used by foresters to mark a trail. Then we looked, every 100 to 300 feet, to find the next. And then we did. Yreka !

So, now we knew we were on a forest trail, hopefully, and not some trail of a mad man, and now it was a game of find the ribbon.

The more we progressed, the more we realized that the trail was expertly made using a high-resolution GPS tracker.

It followed the contour lines perfectly . Lines it was impossible to see because of the high vegetation and dense trees.

During this stage of the trek, Fred was indispensable.

It was impossible to see the ground, so we had to feel our way along it using our sticks.

Early on, I walked into a small lava tube, buried in the high ferns, and was only saved by Fred, from falling into the pit.

Without those red ties, it would have been completely impossible to find our way.

We got to the bottom in early afternoon. The trees thinned and the meadows opened up.

It was truly a heavenly moment. We were probably the first to go there in hundreds of years, besides the forest dept.

Now we could walk freely and follow the cliffs up to the head of the valley, where the magical place we had gazed upon for so many years, would be.

 The signs of pigs were everywhere. We knew, come late afternoon, they would be out in force.

These pigs were huge, 500 to 800 lbs.

They would gladly hunt you and eat you if you gave them half a chance. Many people had been lost in this valley coming in from the ocean side.

We finally arrived at the heart of the meadows, where the cliffs ended and there was a waterfall.

We stood at last in the awe inspiring and forbidden land of our dreams.

There was ice on the rocks where the water came down. There were strange flowers and butterflies and birds of all kinds that I didn't recognize, all around us.

The place seemed thick with life and the unknown. The air

was fragrant with magic and
mist.

It was filled with the mystery and
the danger.

We wanted badly to just lay down
in the meadows by the falls, and
dream. But we were very aware
of the limited time we were being
allowed to hang out in the magic.

The guardians were returning,
and very soon.

So, we made our offerings of
prayers and medicine and food
and began our journey back.

The light had shifted, and not to
our advantage. It was very hard

to find the ribbons. That is the moment Fred came to life.

Finding ourselves hopelessly stuck, I held up Fred, almost as a joke and said "ok Fred, which way.?"

Suddenly he just twirled in my hand and faced back. So, I said "alright," and turned back and walked a few steps down, and sure enough, there was the red tie I had missed.

Well, after that we were both believers, and Fred led us out with 100 percent accuracy every time.

We really could not have made it in the growing dusk.

The pigs were already celebrating the coming feast. And we would be the guests of honor.

 Fred led us home, and not for the last time either.

Now that we knew about his deeper side, we were not afraid to make us of it.

 He never failed us. What can be said of such a friend. He has been eternally true.

There is another side to Fred, that is more difficult to explain. I knew right from the beginning, that Fred had been some

Kahuna's or medicine man's walking stick.

 He just had to much manna in him.

The fact that he was placed deeply into a pool that was very narrow and hard to dive into, told me he was put there for safe keeping.

I have had two distinct visions, that would often repeat, during my time with him.

   The first was of a place that I tried for 20 years to get to. It was the area that lay next to the Eke crater. It was almost completely inaccessible, filled to the brim with hidden lava tubes and many

tunnels and treacherous falls. It
was also filled up with the
remains of the Menehune on
Maui.

    They were known as the little
people. You would never see
them, unless they wanted you to.

 These are an actual people
descended from the original
Aboriginals that inhabited Maui
for probably thousands of years.

    I knew of several people who
had run into them, deep in the
mountains. One woman, I knew
lived with them on Kauai for
about a month in a very remote
area.

They were a very small people,
maybe four feet tall at the most.

They were completely covered with hair, very similar to Big Foot.

They seemed to be capable of multi-dimensional travel . They have never been officially discovered for obvious reasons. I knew of one case at least, where a climber had fallen deep into a lava tube. He had broken his leg and passed out.

He woke up in the morning, and he was out, and his leg had been mended.

 There was no one around him anywhere. This was in the area where the little people seemed to hang out.

There are local families who have made relations with them over the years, but no white people have ever been introduced with the exception of the woman who lived with them for a month.

They were known by the locals as the torch bearers, because when they came out, they were seen carrying a long line of torches.

The locals were very afraid of them most of the time.

A local man, who is about my age, remembers his granny grabbing him by the arm when he was about five and rushing him into the house, when the torch bearers came out. (That would be Maui in the fifties.)

They were considered magical
and dangerous.

These were the visions I would
get when I would walk with Fred
in the West Mountains. I would
see a world filled with menehune
all around me.

Menehune all living in deep lava
tubes and caves, in the area next
to the Eke.

A world I had never imagined.

The next vision is even more
difficult to describe.

It is about a realm of beings, that I
have never even dreamed of.

In my ongoing search for an easier access to the Eke creator, I took a long back road, that seemed , on the map, to be gentler.

I hiked all day with two other friends. It was not an easy hike, and we were completely exhausted by the time we had finally reached the swamp, and the cliffs that led to the Eke.

The sight that we saw when we got there, haunts me still.

We finally arrived in the evening light. Everything was still visible, but the light was dim.

I gazed up and saw before me a rising ridgeline of heavily forested cliffs, coming out of a swamp, that was deep and went on for miles. It was only a few hundred feet to the first land fall, but we brought no raft to cross over.

What I was so struck by, was the intensity of the feeling that was radiating off those cliffs.

It was not a dark energy, but it very clearly was a **do not come here**, just blasting forth , across the water at us.

There was nothing normal about any of this. It suddenly went from a hike to the Eke, to crossing over into another realm all together.

It was a realm that was most assuredly forbidden to us at that moment. We could all feel the effects.

There was nothing for it but to make our bedrolls and go to sleep. We were all very tired.

I lay close to the water and just gazed up at this

Indescribably haunting landscape. Very Erie and provoking.

To my surprise, I fell quickly asleep, and found myself still gazing up at the strange new world even in my dream.

Even though my body was asleep, I was very awake and deeply thrilled by what I saw.

What I saw, were literally
hundreds of bodies of people, all
lined up in rows, and all inside the
cliffs, and even it seemed, sort of
under them. They were not
ghosts or spirits, and they were
all totally luminous.

I could not make out their
faces, but I could see their human
form. I had no idea what I was
looking at.

A legion of luminous souls. They
seemed to be conscious and
aware of me, but I had no contact.

I gazed at them all night, trying to
make out what it was I was
actually witnessing.

It was almost like I had a
window into another world. I
couldn't be sure if they could see
me or not. If they could, they
weren't in a rush to let me know.

They seemed very bright and
alive, but to busy to be bothered
by me.

And yet, there was no physical
movement. The movement was
all mental. I was just some kind of
strange anomaly, that could view
their reality, but had no clue what
I was seeing.

 Their brightness was astounding.
I had never even imagined such a
light body.

The whole scene was so unbelievable, I finally just passed out, and went into a kind of dream time that I have no memory of.

In the morning, it was still stunning and vastly beautiful and yet, completely un- approachable.

That much was very apparent to us. We simply were not invited. It would have been impossible for us at any rate. If we had had a boat, I would dearly have liked to explore the swamp.

 But it was so foreboding

And weird,

We hung about just taking it all in for a long time, before we began our long journey back home.

The image that remained with me was of a deeply luminous world, filled with beings that I really could not understand.

It haunted me and tantalized me at the same time. I have never forgotten the moment of stunning brightness and strangeness .

Who was I looking at? What was I seeing. I know it was no dream. But whatever it was, it was beyond my comprehension.

Very exciting, and very confusing. A lot like my life in general.

Whenever I would hike in the west mountains with Fred, this memory would come back clear and hard. Somehow this was connected to Fred.

The best I could come up with was that I was seeing into the afterworld of the Menehune. I knew Fred was connected to them.

My being able to see them was somehow connected to him. It was like it was actually he, who was seeing them, and I was just along for the ride.

The world of the Menehune was very real to me, but it simply made no sense to my conscious mind. I could feel a great deal, but with no understanding at all.

Perhaps what I was feeling was Fred's love and yearning for a reality that no longer existed.

At least not in the present time. The memory did have the feeling of another time, and something that was enduring in a completely different reality.

The dream time of the Menehune, how on earth did I manage that one.

A shaman's world is often very strange, and completely not understandable to anyone else. Hence the reason for my long silence.

My friends and I never talked about that experience. As far as they were concerned, it was best forgotten.

But what a shame, to forget about something so astoundingly beautiful and completely weird.

I had another Eke moment with Fred, some years later. I was gazing up at it from the closest viewpoint from the road, which was surprisingly close.

I noticed something moving on the top, close to the edge. I took out my binoculars and had a look.

Before my eyes, quite clearly and in total focus, was a large creature. It looked completely like some kind of tetradactyl .

From the distance of a least a mile away, it must have been over 50 feet long. It was all black and shiny. Had no feathers or any other markings.

Then suddenly it just rose up and glided effortlessly into the swamp, four thousand feet below.

And no, I was not on any mind-altering substances .

Was I amazed? that would be putting it mildly. I never spoke to anyone about it except my son, when he was older.

If I was stupidly rich and bored, would I mount an expedition to explore the huge and completely inaccessible swamp below the Eke?

I would in a heartbeat. That's where the real lost world is hiding out. And there is every good chance it will stay that way for a very long time.

To a shaman, the world is always a mysterious place.

Full of the unknown and the
sublime, and always dangerous to
ignore.

If you follow the medicine
way, it will always reveal to you
the hidden truth behind the mask
you have made for yourself,

It is always bringing you to light,
and usually through sorrow and
pain.

But the joy is inescapable and
strong and difficult to ignore.

And the fun can be outrageous.

It is always a balancing act. If
you manage somehow to keep
your equilibrium and your
openness,

You will always be in the rising vortex of life's blessings.

The light is always eager to sign you up for more work, if you say Yes.

Never easy, but usually amazing and spectacular at he very least.

Here is a story of a mother's love, that still makes me cry, when I remember .

Mother Bear

I was hanging out in Yosemite Valley, in the climbers' camp, with Patrick, and we were hoping to find some real rock climbers to teach us the basics

We had already spent a month in the high country at Thousand Island Lake, but the snow had finally come, and we retreated to the valley.

It was very pleasant and sunny, and I was spending most of my time watching the bears.

We had hung our packs, as instructed by all the guidebooks, up high in a tree, as the only safe way to keep them from bears.

The guidebooks did not say anything about a mother with two cubs, however. Two very hungry cubs.

The first day we arrived we hung our packs very carefully, as we were getting low on food.

Very secure and tidy or so we thought. I arose early in the morning to watch the bears.

This particular mother and cubs had caught my interest.

I hid out with a view of the packs and watched.

327

When the bears arrived on the scene, the mother casually walked over to the trunk of the tree and sent the cubs up the tree.

They immediately got to work and climbed out on the long branch the packs were hanging from and started to swing them on the rope.

As the arc of the swing got larger and larger, the packs came close to the trunk and the mother simply reached over and swiped them with her claws when they were in range, and most of the food just fell to the ground.

It was of course, immediately eaten by the cubs. I watched in disbelief as a week's worth of food disappeared into the mouths of two small bears.

I managed to salvage the remains, but I soon realized we had been easily outsmarted by the bears.

I spent the next week just following them and watching them raid all the packs that had been carefully hung, according to protocol .

They were extraordinarily clever bears. I developed a real fondness for them, and the mother seemed to understand that I was no threat.

Early one morning as I was watching them in a grove overlooking the river, I came a little to close.

The mother immediately responded. She dropped to the ground with her chest and made a low roar. Then she looked me in the eye and slowly moved towards me.

I understood, and slowly just moved back. When I was about 60 feet away, she stopped and told me that was the line I must not cross.

From then on, I was careful to always keep the boundary she had set for me.

The next morning, we were at the same site over the river, when the mother suddenly froze and chased the cubs up the nearest tree.

I was surprised, and I went to look down, and there was a huge male bear walking up the river.

Now male bears will often eat or kill cubs that are not theirs. The problem was that the cubs would not stay in the tree for long, without going to look for their mother, if she left.

The mother had a real problem. So, despite her better instincts, she decided to enlist my help.

She walked right over to me, only a couple feet away, and looked me deeply in the eyes.

She asked me very plainly to watch her cubs, and keep them up in the tree, and not to let them come down under any circumstances.

I was deeply touched that she would trust me, but I understood the desperate nature of the situation.

I simply bowed to her and said yes, I would be glad to be the bear sitter for as long as it took.

Then she looked at me again and said that I must keep the boundary she had given me .

Then she waited until I again agreed to the terms of the arrangement.

Once the deal was made, she ran off immediately to lead the male bear as far away from her cubs as possible.

The minute she left; the cubs started to climb down.

I immediately assumed my duties and gave a shout and clapped my hands vigorously until they went back up the tree.

They were very surprised, but they seemed to know that I was under instructions from the mother.

This little bear dance went on for at least three hours, with the bears trying to get down every 20 minutes or so, and me as the bear sitter jumping in and screaming and clapping until they went back up.

The cubs didn't really know what to make of this, and they kept testing me to be sure I was serious. But I held firm and did not relent .

333

So, there they were when the mother at last returned. The very first thing she did was to smell all around to see if I had kept my distance.

After she had satisfied herself of my integrity as a bear sitter, she came over and looked me deeply in the eyes and thanked me from the bottom of her heart.

The emotion and the gratitude were very apparent to me, and I was deeply touched and honored by her response.

Then she went and got the cubs down, who both were very curious about me, and lead them away at a fast pace.

I stood awhile and just wept. I had never received such love from anyone before. I was deeply moved.

I must have earned my bear badge that day, because ever since that moment between us, all bears have always treated me with the utmost respect.

It was a turning point in my understanding about

how love can go beyond all barriers of form and function.

Deep love just goes beyond all reason and even instinct.

I have never forgotten that moment. I will Cherise it

Forever. My heart grew stronger for it.

And I was the better man.

The Wilderness Enlightenment Intensive

It has almost been forty years since that unique and extraordinary event graced my life.

When I thought back, I realized that there was never a better example in my life at least. Of the medicine wheel in action.

This was to be the culmination of my career as an enlightenment master. It was probably the bravest thing I ever did, at least, as far as working with people went.

The enlightenment intensive was created by Charles Berner,

who later became my guru, and was known as Yogishwar Muni. He was the first one to put me on the path, so to speak.

The intensive itself was based on the ancient Zen practice, known as a Zen Sishen. This is a thousands of years old, and extremely difficult form of meditation.

Yogishwar took the same format and added a communication part to the sitting contemplation.

He realized that most western people would get totally lost in a koan type contemplation.

A koan, is an impossible question that has no logical answer. It is something you have to come to by awakening, and not by any mental reasoning. An example of a koan would be "who am I ." In the zen tradition they would often use "what is Mu", or "what is the sound of one hand clapping."

There are many koans in the zen tradition, and each one represents a stage of enlightenment, or awakening that the participant must come to.

The format of a Sishen was very severe.

You would awaken at six am and have fifteen minutes to get ready for the first sitting. The sitting was usually forty-five minutes long, and then there would be a five minute break, and then you would start again. This would go

339

on for 18 hours, usually until midnight. Then you would collapse into your bed roll, usually on the floor, and start again at six in the morning.

There would be short breaks for meals, all vegetarian, and short walks and a brief working contemplation. There were no distractions allowed of any kind. No coffee, or stimulants, no sex, no nothing.

This would go on for 72 hours in the traditional format.

In the Zen world, you would have to sit in full lotus, back very straight, and if you ever slouched or nodded off, a man with a very large stick would hit you very hard on the back. But he would only hit you on very special points in order to help you to stay awake.

Sitting in full lotus, means your legs crossed in front of you, and your feet resting on your legs. It is a very painful position, if you are not used to it.

The point is to keep your back very straight, and to keep your mind very alert.

In the Renzi world of Zen, the participants would sit in a row and face each other. This is the model that Yogishwar adopted.

In the early days, the EI's were very rigorous. There were no comforts of any kind. You slept on the floor, the schedule was strictly followed, there was no talking or chit chat.

When I arrived back from England, in the late 70's

I discovered Yogeshwar, and began doing the intensives. I did many 3 day, and several two week intensives and some 5 day.

A two week would literally cook your mind.   You would not be the same afterwards.

I found that I had a gift for the process, and after 5 years, Yogishwar told me to do the master's training, which he would be giving.

The training was very tough. Yogishwar had written a 300 page manual, which you basically had to memorize, followed by a lot of severe kind of crises management tests.

Becoming and Enlightenment master was difficult, but not the same as becoming a zen Roshi, which takes a lifetime.

The beauty of the intensive was that you didn't have to be a Roshi. The process was enough.

The job of the master was just to keep the participants doing the technique correctly, and to keep everyone awake and focused. It was more about inspiration and crises management.

The part that YM had added was about communication.

The forty-five minutes was divided into 5 min dyads. You would spend 5 min as the contemplating partner, and 5 min as the listening partner, and then a bell would ring, and you would change over.

 The contemplating partner would, after a minute or two, do their best to communicate what had come up for them during their contemplation.

Then they would continue their contemplation.

   Yogishwar knew very well that few westerners could actually do a single focus meditation, like. who am I, without just following their mind around through all the memories and stories.

344

Koan contemplation is very rigorous. You had to stay with the focus, and only with the focus.

The focus was to become directly aware of who you are, outside the mind and personality.

When you intended to do that, then something would arise. It could be a memory, or a backache, or a thought.   He knew, that if someone were to communicate that process to another, then it would leave the mind, and the person would then be free to focus on their koan again.

The secret was to stay focused only on the koan, like who am I, and be open to experiencing the direct event of that, outside of the mind.

Turns out the process works very well. It was very hard to stay with it of course, but if you could persevere, the mind would collapse after about two days, and you would have a good chance of having a genuine enlightenment.

What was a good indicator of having an enlightenment?

It was not all the energy that would be released, which was something to behold.

It was like crossing through a jungle, trying to find the trail, and being hopelessly lost. Then suddenly you are standing 500 feet above the jungle, and you can see the trail, and all the surroundings and everything that you needed to know in order find your way.

The apparently very hidden and mysterious, would become suddenly self-evident. That was the real clue.

It was not about an inspiration, or a realization. It was much deeper. It was an actual change in your consciousness. Now you knew who you were.

Often you could not really describe the experience very well, because it was not really an experience at all. It was an event of a change of consciousness that would be permanent. It would not just fade into a memory.

Of course, there are many levels of this event.   Some were very large and earth shattering, and some were just a wonderful kind of A Ha.

But they were all a permanent change in your awareness. And that is the difference between an insight, and an enlightenment.

At any rate, I found I had a gift for this. Not just in the taking, but also in the giving. It was my true life's work. I loved it, and I was very good at it.

So, I went on to give many 3-day intensives, then 5 day then 7 day, then 2 weeks. I had given two of the two-week intensives, and I was amazed at there power to change lives.

I basically did this for five years, before I decided to add a shamanic element to it all.

I came up with the idea for the wilderness intensive. It was radical, and completely impossible, but I knew I had to do it.

I decided on Mt Shasta, in California. So, I began to talk to the forest rangers for permission.

Turns out, it was completely out of the question.

First of all, no one was allowed up on Mt Shasta, due to logging.

It was the dry season and the fire season. Camping was only allowed for a few days, with a small amount of people, and absolutely no fires would be allowed.

The areas for camping were very restricted, and very public.

This was not at all what I wanted.

So, I worked my way up the totem pole of rangers, until I came to the last one, who was the very head of the department. He was the boss.

I managed to get an interview with him, which was no small miracle to begin with.

I spent the morning trying to explain to him about

enlightenment intensives, and what it was I wanted to do.

I had basically 16 people that I wanted to take into the wilderness around Mt Shasta, including my wife and small daughter, and keep them out there for 4 or 5 weeks, and do all our cooking on open fires. Completely outrageous.

To my complete surprise, the man listened very carefully to my long and elaborate explanation, then he told me quietly to just follow him and get in his truck.

I was very surprised, as you can imagine.

He told me that what I wanted
was against all rules and
regulations, but that he had the
power to make it happen.

He was a deeply spiritual man, as
it turned out, and understood
what it was I was trying to do.

He said we couldn't talk about
it in his office, but he was going to
take me to a place where the
event could happen.

He said Mt Shasta was out of
the question, for many reasons.
But the older mountain that was
just below Mt Shasta, Mt Eddy had
a wonderful view of the mountain
and was located near a lake. The
lake was named, Toad lake.

It turns out that Toad Lake was an ancient Native American village site. It was loaded with arrow heads, and lots of Manna.

That was the place, he said, and he would work out the details with the forest dept.

It took us about an hour or more of driving in his four-wheel drive truck, over rough roads, but then we arrived.

I was completely blown away by the beauty and the energy of the place. It was deeply enchanted.

I looked at him and I almost wept. He only laughed and patted me on the shoulder.

He said he would trust me to not burn down the forest, or do anything stupid, and that I had to be very careful of bears and large animals.

He said he would have to come up with quite a story to get me a waver for the event from the forest dept, which was a very conservative dept.

He said he could make it happen, and he would , but only if I gave him my solemn word that I would do my very best to be as careful as possible, and not create any problems for him.

I almost went down on my knees to thank him. I really did not know what to say.

There were no words really, it was all just the grace of the Great Spirit, moving through two like-minded men, who found each other on opposite sides of the river.

I often wondered if there was a past life connection between us. It was almost like a secret alliance made between two opposing generals, that did a world of good and was completely unknown to the rest of the world.

Nevertheless, now I was set. I had a place, I had permission from the top, and I was ready to move forward.

After that impossible miracle, everything fell together very quickly. In no time at all I had ten people willing to risk their lives, a heroic staff, and we were off to the lake.

The important thing to understand about a medicine wheel, is that it truly is a wheel.

Everything and everyone are of equal importance on the wheel. Even though the events , especially the shamanic events were extraordinary, I was only doing my part in a very large picture.

The larger picture that I learned to understand and appreciate, *was that the forces of life all come together to support and inspire the search for truth, when it is sincere.*

Toad Lake was a magnificent and a perfect place for us. The lake was beautiful and enchanting. The water was clean. All around us was deep wilderness.   There were no other people or even roads to get to us. The only road was an extreme four-wheel drive which no one used.

It took us a week to set up the camp.

All cooking was done over an outdoor fire pit that was nestled in a group of crystalline boulders that simply vibrated with power.

Our lodge was an old parachute, very large, but of course not waterproof. There was never any rain that time of year, especially during the dry season.

I brought along some large plastic tarps, just in case.

We had to build a sweat lodge, that was a real sweat lodge. No plastic or synthetic materials could be used.

Then there was the problem of wood.

We had to burn a huge amount of wood to heat the stones for the lodge. It took at least 3 hours to heat the large stones to a red-hot state. The fire had to be large and continuous.

My senior monitor, whose name was Jerry Leach, was primarily responsible for this monumental task. We all helped of course in wood gathering, but we could use no power equipment because of the noise. Everything had to be cut by hand. Many cords of wood had to be gathered and cut. The fire was large and almost continuous. And all this in the middle of a very dry forest during the fire season. The mindfulness required was almost apocalyptic.

My dear friend Murray, who was a part of the intensive, told me later that he had never seen anyone work as hard as Jerry did during those 5 weeks. It was almost superhuman.

Jerry was the fire man. Then there was the cook. At the heart of any medicine wheel, there is always the food. Our cook was named Namrata. She was probably the most spiritually sincere woman I have ever known.

She lived only to serve others. She asked nothing in return. Everything was always prepared with love and great care.

The food was fresh and wholesome, and the energy she emanated was always just radiant.

The intensive would never have been what it was, without her. She was the shining deva at the heart of it.

I am hoping that by now, she is the reverend mother at a Zen monastery.

Then of course, there was
Murray. Murray had taken every
one of my intensives. He was like
the drum that beat out the
heartbeat. Always true, always
filled with truth. His presence
made all the difference. Probably
the real reason my other
intensives had been so successful,
with such a high percentage of
people achieving a direct
experience, was because of
Murray.

He always set the tone. And it
was always a very high tone.

Since that time, he has gone on
to give intensives for forty years,
nonstop.

He is still giving them today.
He has given more than any other

Enlightenment Master in the world .

So, I was indeed fortunate in my friends and staff. The wheel was set, and after a week we were ready to begin.   We had no electricity or power, so we relied entirely on day light.

We started early, usually by six am. We followed the same schedule of walks and meals and working contemplation. By the early evening, we stopped for the sweat lodge.

Early on in my life as a master, I discovered that combining sweat lodge with an intensive was a very good idea.

Western people tend to get very mental in their approach to meditation. Experienced meditators especially. These people were all experienced.

But no one is prepared for a real sweat lodge experience. When they are hot, and mine were very hot.

The body will go into a crisis. You think you cannot breathe. You think you are going to die or be burned alive.

The only way through is to just surrender and let it all go and wait for death to drag your shriveled body outside.

Mental defenses did not work. It was all physical.

So, I found the perfect way to push people into a crisis, who otherwise would never go there.

They were used to the mental crises. But they were not used to being roasted alive and suffocated in a sweat lodge.

I was truly in my element. After a while, everyone realized that they were not going to die, and could relax . When you could finally relax, an amazing thing would happen. Suddenly you felt like everything was all right and the crises would pass.

Now the stone people could go to work on you and heal you with the steam and with their songs and blessings. I never knew what I was going to sing or say. It would all just flow through me. It was always perfect.

After about a week into the intensive proper, I was singing in the sweat lodge and suddenly a rain song came out of me. I knew it was a rain song, but I didn't know how I knew.

 Sure enough, the next morning it began to rain. It rained for seven days and nights.

   We of course were barely prepared for any rain. We managed to get the plastic tarps up and secure the lodge, but just barely.

   Now, every day, twice a day, we would go out for walking contemplation. I would beat my drum to signal the time for the walk, and then the rain would stop.

I was stunned and delighted. Not at all what I was expecting.

When everyone came back in, I would beat the drum again, and the rain would start.

Every day, twice a day, this would happen.

Even though it was amazing to watch, I felt like it was just the thunder beings trying to do their part to help out. I didn't really take it personally.

That is how the medicine wheel works, everyone just does their part.

Keeping the fire going was the real trick. Somehow Jerry

managed to keep the fire just hot enough and big enough to be able to heat the rocks up.

It was another minor miracle. And Namrata managed to do all the cooking, in the rain.

   Another element to the intensive, everyone, was expected to do a vision quest during the night.

They could decide when, but it had to be done.

The vision quest was a walk into the dark and up a cliff, a very high cliff, with no light. You had to pick your place and meditate all night without sleeping. No food was allowed. Only water.

The night you would go up, the group would give you a rousing send off with singing and chanting around the fire.

Then off you would go up with no lights and only your bed roll.

The climb up the cliff was steep and in the total dark. By grace alone, no one was hurt. In fact, there were no injuries of any kind for the whole intensive.

Even though there were large animals around, they gave us a distance and their blessing. Even the birds and the snakes and the bugs.

It was a true medicine wheel. It was a living and breathing event at the core of it.

Finally, we came to the end, and the sun came out.

It was a heroic day all around. We all went swimming in the lake and Namrata prepared a feast.

When I looked up at the thunder beings in order to thank them for their help, I noticed a very amazing sight, just above out lodge.

There was the absolute perfect form of an ancient chief. He was just smiling down upon us.

I gathered the group, and we all saluted him and gave a song.

I was quite blown away. The likeness was so perfect, it was almost like a photograph.

He stayed around for many hours and gave us

His continual blessing. He was very large. He was the size of a vast cloud, and there was no mistake about it. The whole place seemed to be filled with his presence.

I was jubilant to have such a confirmation of our event.

I have never seen anything like that, before or since. It was the perfect end to a very unique moment in our lives.

All the animals, and even the birds seemed to appreciate the scope of the moment.

The medicine wheel was indeed dancing before us in glee and gratitude.

It took us a week to take it all down and clean up.

After it was all over, I took several of us down to thank the ranger for all he had done.

And specially to let him know that all was well, and the camp was secure.

We were all glowing. There was actually light coming out of us.

He took one look at us and just laughed.

"You see," he said, "I was right to let this happen."

Then he gave me a book that was most precious to him. It was intitled," *The Jungian Senoia Dreamwork Manuel .*"

This was the book, he said , that had changed his life.

It was truly an honor to be given such a book from him, and I received it with deep gratitude.

We left his office in the full knowledge that a good and a deep work had just been done by all.

He was just as much a part of the wheel, as any of us.

We were all just doing our part in the continual dance of the Great Spirit, on the wheel that never stops.

   After that event, I truly realized that to be a shaman, was not really such a personal thing after all.

The rain had come, because the stone people had given me a rain song.

The place was in drought, and the rain was needed badly.

I was in a somewhat magical position, chanting in a real stone lodge, and so they made use of me.

My experience with mother bear, was a similar kind of situation.

I just happened to be in a place where I could help.

We think we are in control of this life, and by all appearances we seem to be.

The older I get, the more I
understand. We are only a dancer
on the wheel. We dance to the
music that is before us, and our
feet are driven by truth, as we are
driven by the love of truth.

The only thing that is really
happening, is that the compassion
of the Eternal One is slowly
burning away the illusion of
separation.

We burn in a fire, we cannot see

We swim in the Sea of God

All we can really do, is to say Yes

.

And then we rise

And even if we say No

We can only stand the suffering
for so long

The pain and the sorrow will bring
us home again

Back to where it all began.

Jai Ram   Jai Jai   Hanuman

all right now

you can't get away that

easily

This is a book of poetry after

all.

Rest in Truth

Seek not to sully your blade

With the blood of fools

They will always bring an end

to themselves

Seek the truth within

It abides nowhere else

Rest always

In the simplicity of joy

That brings the truth to light

Bath in this and refresh your
soul

Beingness is all around you

Above you and below you

You cannot avoid it

Even if you try

There is no enemy on the
outside

There is only the truth

Within

THE END

THE END

THE VERY END

INDEED

Seek no further

Oh child of the

wind

Jai Ram

Authors Biography

Andrew Quilliam Brewer aka
(Jaya Deva}

Is a very simple sadhu and poet

He lives with his son,   And the
last, and I mean the very last, of
a true pack of large dogs

And a Murderous cat ,

in the hills of Western North
Carolina.

He considers himself to be a
champion of the small, and he is
devoted to the revelation of the

Eternal that all beings, and all

form, dwell within, and without.

He is quite willing to dazzle, if

he must, and even go further still.

He sees the magic, and he knows

the grace

That abounds in all life. And he

will not stop bringing forth the

shine

Until it smiles, within .

Jai Ram

Once again,   the quantum spark
Just refuses to play nice

What's to be done, after all

Well, here it is   the final word
from

The Diary of the <u>dawn</u>

dancer

The Cup of Heaven

This is a realm that is real

It is made from love

It is made by the grace of the
amazing and enduring

Memory of light.

This is a scientific fact, photons
have memory

If at any time you have deeply
loved, does not matter the who, or
the what, can be from a simple
friendship, or just from acts of
random goodness, you can drink
from this cup.

It turns out that light is created
by goodness, and it remembers all

goodness and love. If your subtle eyes have been opened, you can see this.

It is created by a leap that arises in the heart, very similar to photosynthesis.

This leaping is part of the creation cycle. It changes the heart and charges the photons.

 Now, the event is recorded by light, in a realm that is outside of times' dominion.   True love is eternal. It dwells in" no time".

So, this is where you may be drawn to at your death, or even while you live.

It is a realm that is filled with goodness, and light.

385

It is more real than any darkness, which is just ignorance, that you may be carrying unwittingly, on your back.

Here is where you may abide instead and go through the cycles of completion that are inherent in all cycles.

Those would be the healing cycles of the heart, and they can take you to where you need to go.

So here you may rest and grow stronger.

This realm is accessible to anyone.

It does not require any belief, or religion.

It requires only the event of real love and goodness.

It turns out that true events, filled with a presence of love and goodness, will endure, just as we endure.

Love is never lost
It is always remembered by light

True love endures forever, as do we.

Believe what you like, beliefs mean nothing to reality.

It is what you do, and how you are
in your beingness , that means
something.

It is your birthright as a human
being, to come home at last.

If only you will

So, home you may come to rest if
you want, in this unique realm.

This realm is all about healing and
bringing your life into balance.   It
is not about judgement or blame.

It is about bringing the cycles of
love into completion.

And then you can start again, on
your quest for awakening.

Jai Jai Hanuman

The door to this realm is opened
by the love of truth

Without any conditions.

Unconditional love of truth, will
take you there,

And your memory of real events

You may have almost forgotten
them , but even a little bit will do

To light the fire, again.   Jai
Ram just remember yourself

If only you will.

Well, we almost made it to
the end of the final end

and now of course, the dung
beetle would like to be the
very end.

He is famous afterall

Must be a bug thing, to be at
the very end of the final end

and I must confess, I do
enjoy his story

The dung beetle's story

Allah Bantha Ezrahiem!!!! cried the beetle with great feeling. He was hoping to impress the spider, and by some miracle, he did.

The spider quickly pushed him from the web. "I will not drink the blood of zealots and fanatics" she cried, "be gone."

Now the beetle, much to his amazement, found himself free of the web, and he hurriedly ran away to live another day, hurray!

From that moment on, he became a reformed bug. He changed his name to Allah Bantha and sang prayers every morning to God. This was the humble beginnings of the famous beetle poet and reformist, Allah Bantha Ezraheim.

Now, the truth is, the poor old dung beetle was never a zealot or fanatical in the least. He was very creative, and he loved his life dearly, but he never knew why those particular words just came

rushing from his mouth, with such
intensity.

"Perhaps," he mused, "he was
saved by one of his past lives,
when he was fanatical and a
zealot,

hence the reason for his present
life as a dung beetle."

When he was later born as a
man again, he realized that every
life has a purpose and a meaning.
And when later, he won the
Pulitzer Prize for poetry, he
understood his strange journey,

a little better.

And he never forgot his life as a
dung beetle, and a zealot, and
possibly even, once, as a spider

Is everybody happy now? Well
alright then

The end
the end

The final end

and hurray for that

The end indeed

Lord Narayana Jaya

Lady Lakshmi   Jaya

Jaya to Hanuman

And to Saraswati

Jaya Jaya   Jaya Ram

"The truth upholds the
fragrant earth and makes the
living waters wet.

   Truth makes the fire burn,
and the air move, makes the
sun shine, and all life grow.

A hidden truth supports
everything   find it and win."

(From the Ramayana, as retold by
William Buck)

fini

And then of course
There is always the Real

What if the real mystery of life
Is not about consequences
Or gain or lose
It is about
Finally getting it   right

And we go   and we do
and we seek
But we don't know who we are

And then we follow our
attractions and our desires

And we suffer and we suffer
And we suffer

And all that we gain
We lose
And all that we learn
That is not real
We forget
And then we start again

Until our present cycle

Of love and desire

Gets fulfilled and completed

And that is the real

Healing cycle of the heart

We go

Until we can finally forgive
ourselves enough to allow

Awakening   to occur

Then we can let go

Of all our desires that
continuously feed the illusion

Of our life

And know

It is only the real self

The Atman at the core

That is the treasure

That we seek

And when it is finally found

Desire and suffering and

Duality

all vanish

and we stand in the Real

at last

and then we can begin again

Well of course there are more
poems, all wanting to move into
the light. So, I have chosen
two more out of the many, and
this must be the end.

Into this wonder, we arise

Softly and gently

Unknown to ourselves

All that we have ever been

We have forgotten

Sadly, we remember only

moments

Like a splash of color

Thrown in hast, upon the wall

From out the madness of

Creations flurry

To be forever real

This is our prayer

This is our dream

And then, one day

We awaken

Oh my, we say

Oh my

And now
The very last poem almost

Rubies and mist

Rubies and mist

Deep runs the waterfall

Of my soul

And I am naked

Revealed to all but myself

I am forever falling into the
river that flows to the ocean

My boat slowly turning into
dust

My wings

Starting to grow at last

The falcon smiles

To watch his dinner

Learning to fly.

The green leopard rose up

And smiled

Teeth glistening in the glad

And happy dawn

At last, she was free

Free from all care

Free from all sorrow

And it was a sunny day

A good day to have died

She breathed in the gracious
light

And knew

Everything was just fine

Just the way it was

Perfection was deep

In the dazzle

That swirled around her

And danced a wild

And a bright and sunny

Song

Her soul was filled with

The beauty of her own

Good heart

And all was as it should be

finito

amigos

aloha

compadres

please
just get it right

this time

www.ingramcontent.com/pod-product-compliance
Lightning Source LLC
Chambersburg PA
CBHW060858140726
47996CB00001B/28